EASY BAKING IN BARB'S KITCHEN

Ho... from Enjoy Love Barb

LOVE BAKING AGAIN!

**ENJOY BEING A HERO
WITH YOUR FRIENDS AND FAMILY,
PERFECTING YOUR BAKING,
IN TIME-SAVING WAYS!**

BARB LOCKERT

Tellwell Talent
www.tellwell.ca

ISBN
978-0-2288-8530-6 (Hardcover)
978-0-2288-8531-3 (Paperback)
978-0-2288-8529-0 (eBook)

Special thanks to the following contributors:

L'CHEF - Exclusive North American Distributor for BOSCH™
kitchen machines and L'EQUIP® products

The Bundy family of American Pan/Bundy Baking Solutions; Premier Pan Company,
Inc. (USA Pan), coordinated by Mike Dandrea, North American Sales Manager

Ventures International Products Ltd., John Newton, President

Barb's Kitchen Centre, Edmonton, Alberta, Canada, local specialty food
store stocking unique, hard-to-kind items, fresh baking and cooking
supplies, and exceptional BOSCH™ and L'EQUIP® small appliances

Photographer & Food Stylist: Heather Muse
Makeup Artist: Jessica Lockert, True Beauty Makeup Artistry

BOSCH™ is a registered trademark of Robert Bosch GmbH, Germany

TABLE OF CONTENTS

INTRODUCTION

Hello, and thank you for picking up this cookbook! My friends call me Barb.

I am a passionate person, especially when it comes to baking, cooking, music, sports and travel! Being a people person with an outgoing personality, I love to spend time with and teach others. There is no higher honour than to share my kitchen with friends and family, especially children, whether in a group setting or one on one. It is my greatest joy to watch children's faces light up from a very young age when they are allowed to help create edible masterpieces. While sharing my enthusiasm, I love the giggles, requests and responses I get in return. We have so much fun, and although they don't know it at the time, they are learning valuable life skills for their future.

Feeding my family and entertaining guests is truly a pleasure. It feeds my soul, and I continually challenge myself to create easy, tasty, healthy recipes. It is a joy to share good food, laughter and memories in my kitchen. I consider this time to be play rather than work.

Who could forget Papa, Walter Hill (my father's father), born in 1900? I remember him explaining how he came to Canada from England in 1913 with his parents and brother. After returning from World War I and graduating from the University of Alberta's first pharmacy class, he went to Fort McMurray, Alberta, in 1922. He then wrote a letter to his friend, Gladys Percy, in England, asking her to come to Canada, and if she still "liked him," they could get married, which they did in 1923. Papa told me how he taught Grandma to cook since "she could not even boil water." She eventually developed healthy cooking skills, thanks mostly to my papa's encouragement and with the help of their large vegetable garden.

When I was growing up, my grandparents lived at the end of the block. I saw them every day when walking to and from school. Their daily lunch was canned vegetable soup, and toasted sharp cheese and ketchup sandwiches. Not the grilled cheese sandwiches we know today, but toasted bread, spread with ketchup and filled with sharp cold cheese. The thought of that combination might have you cringing, but as a young girl nothing was more delicious. I have such fond memories of playing cribbage with Grandma while drinking weak instant coffee loaded with sugar and evaporated milk, and eating treats—*store-bought cookies*—when I stopped by daily after school. I have no personal recollection of Grandma baking anything.

My baking skills were definitely not developed while spending time with Grandma during my formative years. She did, however, have a great sense of humour and enjoyed the companionship of others, even when mistakes were made. Many of my life skills, including baking, were learned by trial and error. When I was a young girl, around six or seven years old, my first cake-baking experience resulted in a brick. I had used the wrong leavening agent. The dog wouldn't even eat it. I learned then that it was okay to laugh at myself. My mom baked often and allowed me to help. My interest increased and my love of baking began!

Lumpy powdered milk was a staple in our house, so it was a treat to have *real* milk at my grandparents' home. Actually, the milk was half canned evaporated milk and half water. Why am I telling you this? This is exactly where my sweet tooth originated. As a child, that milk sure tasted sweet and delicious!

As a parent and grandparent, I believe it is important to teach our young children simple techniques as soon as they are able to stand on a safe chair to assist, rather than grabbing at the counter to see what you are doing. In my kitchen, the rules are quickly learned: wash your hands, put on an apron, and no eating—especially no chocolate chips—until we are finished. Have fun in the process. And we do!

A few comments I have heard often from my children and grandchildren:
    "Grandma, can I help you?"
    "Grandma, can we bake cookies, brownies, doughnuts, etc.?"
    "Can I crack the eggs?"
    "Can I use a mixer?"
    "Can we make that again?"
    "I love helping in the kitchen."
    "Can we eat now?"
    "Can I eat some more?"
    With a gentle nudge from one grandchild: "I remember how to do that!!"

Can you hear their enthusiasm? How can you say *no* to any of these requests?

And the biggest compliments of all:
    "This is GOOD, Grandma. We could make this again!"
    "Can I come back tomorrow?"
    "Grandma, you make everything fun!"

Over the years, I have appreciated all the encouragement from friends who've said, "I want to buy your first cookbook," and "I'm interested in your recipes of a journey in time." Some recipes date back to my childhood and I remember sitting at the kitchen table as a young girl, writing favourite family recipes in a small book which retains a place of honour among my cookbooks today. (See the next section in this book, "The Short Version of a Long Story: Barb's Biography." It explains how I went from childhood to a successful entrepreneur.)

My heart was thumping with excitement when I was invited by Lorraine Mansbridge of Global TV (previously ITV) to present a cooking demonstration on her television show, *Good Good Morning*, which was picked up by satellite for coast-to-coast viewers in Canada. The very first time I walked into the studio with baskets of equipment and food supplies, the realization hit me that this was *live* television. No taping, no mistakes! I couldn't wait to share my passion! Lorraine and I had an immediate connection from that first appearance, in September 1987. At the end of the program, and while the cameras were still rolling, she asked "Will you come back?" Wow! What a compliment! And that was the beginning of more than 33 years of cooking on the air with Lorraine. Our personalities meshed and we became great friends. To this day we continue to bake, share food experiences and ideas, talk endlessly on the phone, and take time to laugh and encourage each other, making memories and bringing so much happiness to us both.

I have had great pleasure designing, organising and hosting numerous culinary tours. It is an honour to host repeat guests and share food experiences while being exposed to cultures in many countries along the way. These travels have added many creative ideas and recipes to my repertoire and satisfy my passion for food and travel. Keep reading to learn more about these tours.

I am sincerely thankful for having the confidence and opportunity *to do what I love* during my teaching and entrepreneur career, and throughout my personal life.

Whatever your age or ability, the purpose of this cookbook is to share my easy recipes, knowledge and life experiences with you. I want you to be comfortable and confident in the kitchen. If this book inspires you to make tastier food, be happier and healthier, then I have accomplished what I set out to do.

Be a hero with your friends and family, and perfect your baking in time-saving ways!

Are you ready? Let's start the music, put on an apron and bake!!!

THE SHORT VERSION OF A LONG STORY: BARB'S BIOGRAPHY

I grew up in Fort McMurray, Alberta, Canada, helping in my grandparents' drugstore (eventually my dad's store), Hill Drugs Ltd. My first introduction to retail was dusting the bottom shelves at the early age of five. Loving numbers, at the age of six, I calculated inventory summaries for the drugstore. I learned very young how to treat others with love, respect, grace and humility.

My grandparents were hard-working, humble, honest, personable and provided great customer service. Developing a strong work ethic and many skills while watching my family serve customers and the community throughout my childhood helped my ongoing success. I looked up to them and credit them for these attributes and have applied them in my life experiences, including owning and operating a retail business. Thanks for being my mentors and teaching me *so* much!

At the age of seven, I received an hourly wage of $0.25. By age 17, my wage had increased to $2.50, and I continued to work on weekend visits during university years.

My love for people and ability to remember individual names has been an asset in every aspect of my life. Determination, confidence, a positive attitude and hard work helped me develop into a strong leader, culminating in receiving prestigious Girl Guide awards: All-Round Cord in November 1971, and Canada Cord in May 1972. I shared my passion, energy and contagious enthusiasm as a leader for Brownies, Girl Guides, sport teams and youth summer camps during my junior and senior high school years.

Deciding not to follow my grandfather's, dad's or brother's footsteps into pharmacy, I attended the University of Alberta in 1975 and received a Bachelor of Education, majoring in Physical Education and Math. I married Tim Lockert in 1979 after two years of courtship and went on to teach elementary school. I was also a contract teacher for several years for the Alberta Correspondence School.

In 1984 I purchased a Bosch Universal Kitchen Machine® and Magic Mill Flour Mill® to save money on our food budget. Using my new kitchen equipment, I developed my own methods to save time when baking. Following extensive research into grain and flour, my priorities were reversed when I realised the nutritional benefits were more important than saving money. Within a few months I began selling bread, squares and muffins at a local farmer's market. My baked goods and 40-loaf supply of bread was quickly exhausted each week.

With retail in my blood, I became a BOSCH™ dealer and began demonstrating and selling Bosch Universal Kitchen Machines®, Magic Mill Flour Mills®, BOSCH™ slicers, dehydrators, stainless steel steam juicers, and food strainers in my home and in the homes of friends. One day, just for fun, I made *Unbelievable Whole Wheat Bread* in five different mixers, as well as in my two-speed Bosch Universal Kitchen Machine®. After the dough was kneaded, from start to finish in my Bosch Universal Kitchen Machine®, it was necessary to transfer the dough from the other machines to my mixer to complete the kneading. This confirmed my confidence in the Bosch Universal Kitchen Machine®. These kitchen machines have a strong motor with transmission, are easy to use and easy to clean.

My exceptional performance and selling success at in-home demonstrations was quickly recognised by BOSCH™ distributors. An opportunity was presented in January 1986. My husband and I were asked to purchase the exclusive distributorship for Bosch Universal Kitchen Machines® and Magic Mill Flour Mills® for Edmonton and Northern Alberta. Today, the mixer and mill are called Bosch Universal Plus Mixer® and NutriMill Flour Mill®.

Thankful for this exciting opportunity, a process began with numerous doors flying open. I was on the right path. Within 62 days, Tim and I incorporated the business, located a storefront, signed a lease, established suppliers and ordered stock. On March 15, 1986, with a four-month-old baby at my side, Bosch Kitchen Centre® in Edmonton, Alberta, Canada, opened for business to sell high-end quality small appliances, practical and unique tools, hard-to-find gadgets, as well as fresh baking and cooking supplies. Tim remained at his place of employment for two years before joining me at the store.

All of this was made possible with borrowed money from my dad (which the bank matched), and I was able to pay back both loans plus interest within a few months, as promised. Speaking of borrowing, I borrowed a skirt suit from my sister-in-law to attend our first convention one month after opening the store. We made it a priority to find solutions to any problems or business challenges. Profits were reinvested to increase inventory.

From the store's inception, I believed it was important to teach customers how to properly use equipment they purchased at our shop. Although I'd had no formal culinary training, I'd had the opportunity to attend and participate in cooking classes in many different countries. My natural and creative teaching ability, clear vision, experiences and professional background enabled me to develop interesting, informative and nutritious cooking classes. I was able to connect personally with customers, and I have been told that my personality, sense of humour and infectious laugh helped generate a family atmosphere.

I often packed up my Bosch Universal Kitchen Machine®, flour mill, countertop oven, baking pans and ingredients for in-class sessions at numerous elementary schools. Milling grain into flour was an eye-opening experience for the children. I made the bread dough and they each had a chance to form a tiny loaf. While the dough was rising and baking, we read *The Little Red Hen* story together. It was exhilarating to see the children, thrilled with their creation, eat their own loaf of bread.

Demonstration-style classes at my store, Bosch Kitchen Centre®, were specifically designed to provide instruction using Bosch Universal Kitchen Machines® and attachments, flour mills, dehydrators, Kuhn Rikon pressure cookers, and innovative and hard-to-find gadgets. Products and fresh baking ingredients sold in the store were promoted while providing valuable information regarding ease of use and efficiency in the kitchen. My focus on *saving time*, *saving money, and retaining nutrition* inspired customers to desire a healthier lifestyle.

While managing the store, I continued my contract teaching position. The business grew rapidly. Within three months it became necessary for me to resign from contract teaching. Before the store's first anniversary, I was ranked the fourth highest volume distributor in North America for BOSCH™ small appliances. A larger location was required by October 1989.

Our second son was born in 1990, and in the midst of raising our two boys and continuing commitments at the Edmonton store, we opened a second Bosch Kitchen Centre® in Red Deer, Alberta, Canada, in 1991, operating and teaching classes for nine years.

Bosch Kitchen Centre®, Edmonton, provided services which included sourcing special requests, European imports, a bridal registry, as well as shipping and warranty repair services for items sold in the store. Our full-service philosophy was very successful and I continued to expand product lines of exceptional quality, durability, reliability and performance, upholding my standard of excellence for the professional and home cook.

Remaining an authorised BOSCH™ retailer, the store name was changed to Barb's Kitchen Centre® in 2012. Some customers did not notice the change for many years. Those customers just knew the store location, regularly attended cooking classes and shopped frequently. One customer admitted, "My car just knows the way"!

It was rewarding to regularly hear positive and encouraging comments from supportive sales representatives and customers about the store, products, and my well-trained staff. Customers returned often to purchase consumables and additional equipment, spreading the word about the store to friends and family.

My planning, organizational skills, attention to detail, and innovative, decisive and progressive thinking demonstrated my commitment to excellence throughout my teaching and entrepreneur career. Intuitive instincts, faith, accomplishments, and personal attributes worked together to create a business that resonated quality and promised strong growth for the company and my personal life.

Continuing the desire to provide ongoing education, I developed a progressive, three-year summer-camp kids' cooking class program to teach life skills to children ten years and older. I am incredibly proud of the hundreds of young people who completed the program and continue to develop their cooking and baking skills. Some attendees came from over 1000 kilometres away. Some have furthered their education at culinary schools.

I was consistently in the public eye through selling products and demonstrating Bosch Universal Kitchen Machines® and Magic Mill Flour Mills® at trade shows and agricultural events, numerous television appearances, and my involvement in helping to organise consumer shows. I networked and shared my expertise through organizations such as Business and Professional Women Alberta and Alberta Opportunity Corporation. I was regularly invited as a feature presenter for Christian women's clubs, ladies' retreats, outreach programs, and church and school groups, including the University of Alberta. Able to present information in an enthusiastic, entertaining and informative manner, I was in demand as a motivational and entrepreneurial speaker for various functions. Volunteering to teach "Kinder Cooking" when our youngest son was in kindergarten was so much fun. Not only was I a prominent business woman, I served in a volunteer role as the board of directors' secretary and camp director for Teen Time of Edmonton for 23 years, reflecting my dedication and community involvement.

Memberships in the Alberta Teachers' Association, Home Economics Council, Retail Merchants' Association of Canada (Alberta) Inc., Red Deer Chamber of Commerce, and my role as a business colleague of Grant MacEwan University proved to be interesting. I mentored business students and published articles and recipes in various magazines and newspapers, including *The Edmonton Home Improvement Book* and *The Red Deer Advocate.*

Imagine my surprise when I began receiving invitations for guest appearances on television programs to provide cooking demonstrations and easy preparation information. After each opportunity, I couldn't wait for the next invitation. I was not nervous, only excited! Back in 1984, I had no idea that making a healthy loaf of bread could be so fulfilling and lead to such adventures!

Appearances and interviews over the years included:

- *ITV Good Good Morning* (before Global) with Lorraine Mansbridge
- *ITV Edmonton Live*
- *ITV Red Deer Getting Together*
- *ITV Red Deer Good Good Morning*
- *ITV Red Deer Live*
- *ITV Red Deer Express*
- *CTV Morning Live Edmonton*
- *CFRN Day By Day* (before CTV)
- *CFRN Alberta Business*

- Access Television, Edmonton, Alberta
- *CKEM TV (A-Channel) Big Breakfast*
- *Breakfast Television*, Edmonton, Alberta
- *Global Edmonton Morning Live*
- *Global Edmonton Morning News*
- *CBC National Marketplace*
- CKRD Radio 7 interview for *World of Women*, Red Deer, Alberta
- CJCA Radio, and many more

These media connections were a blessing, inspired lasting friendships, and the publicity provided excellent business exposure.

More surprises arose when I was recognised as a female entrepreneur by my peers and other professionals. It meant the world to me! I was honoured and amazed to be the recipient of entrepreneur awards, *for doing what I love*, including:

- 1994 Entrepreneur of the Year for the Western Region of Canada (Alberta, Saskatchewan and Manitoba), Retail Category
- 1994 Canadian Women Entrepreneur of the Year for Alberta, in the Quality Plus Retail Category
- 1998 CGTA Retailer of the Year - Honourable Mention
- 2004 YWCA Women of Distinction Award, Entrepreneurs Category

I was surprised to be nominated for many other awards throughout the years, as well.

My love for food and travel influenced my desire to design customised culinary tours of European countries beginning in 2003. These tours were promoted through the store, and customers travelled with me on these adventures. My favourite activities on these tours were, of course, the cooking classes and enjoying culinary delights at every turn. Making pasta from scratch in Italy and Portugal, paella in Spain, apple strudel in Germany, tiramisu in Italy, tarte Tatin in France, topped off with chocolate-making classes in Switzerland and Italy, are some of the mouth-watering experiences that created lasting memories. How many times do you need to travel to Europe? As often as possible!!!

Sharing conversations with locals, learning about their history, and experiencing their culture and magnificent food have led to lifelong friendships. I was also excited to make connections with specialised companies to import and sell their hand-crafted European products. When returning from vacation, instead of sleeping on the airplane, I was often inspired to bake and cook (in my head) and jotted down ideas to create new recipes. It was exhilarating to recreate and taste these creations at home!

While we were on one of the earlier tours, a customer expressed interest in purchasing the store when I was ready to retire. Several years later, the conversation resurfaced, an offer was accepted, and we sold Barb's Kitchen Centre® to a local Edmonton family in October 2019. During the transition, Tim and I assisted the new owners until December 2020.

In my retirement, I spend time with friends, family, travel, design culinary tours, continue to mentor entrepreneurs, and create nutritious, easy and delicious recipes.

Going forward, I will continue to serve and teach others, hoping to influence and inspire good food choices and teach life skills.

I am blessed. Thankful for the tremendous opportunity, I consider it an honour and privilege to have served my customers and friends, far and wide, for over 33 years at Barb's (BOSCH™) Kitchen Centre®, Edmonton, Alberta, Canada.

Enjoy *Easy Baking in Barb's Kitchen*!

Barb Lockert

barb@barbsculinarytours.com

BOSCH KITCHEN CENTRE
- BOSCH APPLIANCES
- FLOUR MILLS
- DEHYDRATORS
- J.A. HENCKELS KNIVES
- BAKING PANS
- BAKING SUPPLIES
- STAINLESS STEEL COOKWARE
- CHOCOLATE MAKING SUPPLIES

9766-51 Cooking Classes 437-3134

World of Women Proudly Presents—

BARB LOCKERT

ENTREPENEUR OF THE YEAR WESTERN REGION "RETAIL"
CANADIAN WOMAN ENTREPENEUR OF THE YEAR
1994 ALBERTA "QUALITY PLUS"

BOSCH KITCHEN CENTRE

DAILY SHOWS:

FRIDAY 5:00 PM & 8:00 PM
SAT 0 PM & 3:00 PM
PM &

GENERAL INFORMATION

Instructions in this cookbook are for use with Bosch Universal Kitchen Machines® to help you save time kneading or mixing. Efficient use of time allows you to enjoy baking more often! These instructions are simple to follow and produce tasty and nutritious products. Each recipe will freeze well and may be multiplied or reduced to suit any lifestyle. A slight adjustment in baking time and oven temperature may be necessary according to elevation. However, all recipes may be mixed manually.

Recipes requesting whole wheat flour refer to grinding hard wheat kernels (berries) into fresh flour in a NutriMill Flour Mill®. Unbleached flour may be substituted in recipes requiring whole grain flour when a flour mill is not available.

ADVANTAGES OF FRESH GROUND (MILLED) WHOLE GRAIN FLOUR

Grinding grain into fresh flour, in a flour mill, provides many benefits:

- It retains nutrition of the grain
- It is wholesome
- It provides natural fibre for health
- It provides texture from the bran and germ
- It enhances flavour and smell in baked goods
- You can mill flour as required
- It is fast and convenient
- It is cost effective

Grains milled into fresh flour do not equate to the kernel measurement. For example: 1 cup (250 mL) hard wheat kernels will yield 1 ½ cups (375 mL) flour.

1 cup (250 mL) soft white wheat kernels will yield 2 cups (500 mL) flour.

Weighing kernels yields the same weight in flour.

Soft white wheat kernels (pastry wheat) may be ground into fresh flour for use in recipes that do not require yeast. This flour creates a whiter baked product with a lighter texture.

Label and store fresh milled flour in a freezer or refrigerator to delay nutrient oxidization, and use at a later date. Personally, I always freshly mill grain for bread making and use the stored flour for other baking. The slight warmth of the flour helps the bread rise.

LET'S TALK ABOUT YEAST

It is personal preference which yeast to use in dough. Recipes in this cookbook refer to instant or active dry yeast and may be used interchangeably. Yeast must be fresh to ensure dough will rise. Storing yeast in the refrigerator or freezer extends the shelf life.

An instant-read thermometer is extremely helpful in bread making to determine the temperature of the liquid, as well as to check the internal bread temperature to ensure the loaves are baked.

When you are unsure how fresh your yeast is, test (bloom or proof) the yeast to confirm it is alive (active) before proceeding: Pour ½ cup (125 mL) lukewarm 110–115°F (43–46°C) water into a small bowl. Add 1 teaspoon (5 mL) of granulated sugar to the warm water. Stir to dissolve the sugar. Sprinkle 1 teaspoon (5 mL) of instant yeast on the water. Use 100–110°F (38–43°C) liquid when checking dry active yeast. Let sit for 5–10 minutes until bubbles form. If no bubbles form, yeast is inactive and new yeast is required. When yeast creates bubbles, you are good to go! Blooming the yeast is always a good recommendation when yeast has been stored a long time.

Bloom yeast for bread dough:

Heat ½–1 cup (125–250 mL) of required liquid amount (water, milk, potato water etc.) to 110–115°F (43–46°C) for instant yeast and 100-110°F (38-43°C) for dry active yeast. Add sugar or desired sweetener to the liquid and stir to dissolve. Sprinkle yeast (according to recipe) on the liquid. Bubbles and foam will appear in 5–10 minutes. Proceed with recipe.

The remaining liquid of the recipe can be heated at 120–130°F (49–54°C) for instant yeast and 105–110°F (40–43°C) for dry active yeast. It is preferrable to bloom (bubble and foam) dry active yeast. Instant yeast is a quick-rise or fast-acting yeast and is much finer in texture than active dry yeast. It is usually mixed directly into dry ingredients and thrives in a warmer liquid atmosphere, which is very warm but not too hot to touch. Having said that, you may dissolve instant yeast in liquid with sweetener before proceeding but is certainly not a necessary step. Dough rises faster using instant yeast and multiple rises are not necessary.

As yeast feeds on sugars and starches inside dough, it converts them into carbon dioxide gases, causing the bread to rise and create an airy, light texture. Cooler liquid temperatures take longer to activate yeast. Liquids too hot will kill yeast. Yeast activity may decrease when in direct contact with salt. Salt in the recipe enhances the flavour.

I am most comfortable with a liquid temperature of 115–120°F (46–49°C) when making breads with instant yeast being added dry to the flour.

Measuring Flour - To measure flour for baking, slowly shake flour from a scoop or cup into an appropriate size of dry measure. Level the excess flour off the dry measure with a bench scraper or flat spatula. Flour becomes compacted in the dry measuring cup when dragged through the flour or the cup is tapped after filling. Incorrectly measured or compacted flour may result in dry, crumbly products. Flour may require sifting before measuring. Read recipe instructions carefully.

When converting recipes from unbleached or all-purpose flour to whole grain flour, reduce whole grain flour by 1 tablespoon (15 mL) per cup in the recipe. This will compensate for germ and bran absorbing the moisture.

Fat - Unless otherwise instructed in a recipe, use softened, room temperature fat such as butter, margarine, shortening or lard.

To cut cold fat into dry ingredients, equip the Bosch Universal Kitchen Machine® with preferred whips. Break the fat into cubes, add to the dry ingredients, cover the bowl and pulse the momentary switch until the mixture resembles small peas.

Scoops - Spring-loaded scoops are useful tools to shape cookies and muffins. To fill, pull the scoop through the batter to the side of the mixing bowl. Squeeze to release the filled scoop into prepared pans. Scoops save time and produce consistent sizes for even baking. Scoops are available in many sizes. Scoop size in these recipes refer to the diameter of the scoop.

Testing Cakes - Cakes and loaves are baked when a cake tester or toothpick, inserted into the centre of the cake, comes out clean. Add additional baking time if batter remains on the tester. Clean the tester after each use or throw away the toothpick.

Oven Racks - For best results, position the baking rack so the baking pans are in the centre of the oven. All levels of oven racks may be utilised when baking in a convection oven.

RISING AND BAKING GUIDE

Dough rising times vary according to the temperature where dough is placed to rise. Baking temperatures are provided in each recipe. However, oven temperatures vary and may require adjusting.

Unbelievable Whole Wheat Bread and *Basic White Bread* loaves may be placed in a 150°F (65°C) oven for the final rise. Most newer ovens cannot be set less than 170°F (75°C). Therefore, warm the oven for 10 minutes at 170°F (75°C), turn on interior light, turn oven off, and place loaves in the warm oven to rise. If available, use the proofing setting to rise yeast doughs.

	Rising	**Baking**
Buns on baking sheet	15 minutes	12–15 minutes
Buns in pan	15 minutes	22–25 minutes
Mini loaves	15 minutes	15–20 minutes
Medium loaves	25 minutes	20–25 minutes
Large loaves	30 minutes	30–35 minutes
		Pizza crust to freeze:
Pizza crust (no toppings)	10 minutes	10 minutes 350°F (180°C)

Cool partially baked pizza crust. Wrap well and freeze.

Top frozen pizza crust with desired toppings. Bake on pizza stone or baking sheet in 425°F (220°C) preheated oven 15–20 minutes until crust is golden brown, depending on pizza thickness.

Pita Pockets – Move oven rack to the top level and preheat to 450°F (230°C). Roll dough thinly on a lightly floured surface, cut as desired, and place on baking sheet. Bake on top level.

| Small pita pockets | (turn pockets over once) | 4–5 minutes |
| Large pita pockets | (turn pockets over once) | 8–9 minutes |

SIMPLE BAKING TIPS

- Unless otherwise stated, eggs are considered large.
- Two egg whites may be exchanged for one whole egg.
- Measure ingredients, such as nuts, after chopping.
- Measure butter after melting unless recipe specifies otherwise.

My hint is to prepare what comes *before the comma* first, such as:
   ½ cup (125 mL) butter, melted.
This refers to *measuring the butter* before melting;
   Whereas ½ cup (125 mL) melted butter
   refers to melting butter to obtain ½ cup (125 mL) of liquid.

- Raisins, cranberries, currants, diced dates, apricots, coconut, nuts, chocolate chips, or yogurt chips may be substituted for each other, depending on flavour and texture desired.
- Dutch cocoa and carob powder may be interchanged.
- Wheat bran and oat bran are interchangeable.
- Chop nuts and seeds in food processor or blender. Pulse to obtain desired consistency.
- Store potato water for breadmaking to add nutrients. Bread will remain soft and moist. Potato flour may be added to bread dough when potato water is not available.
- If you are not satisfied with the results of your bread, cut into cubes for stuffing, bread pudding, croutons, or make into bread crumbs.
- Candied fruits are a tasty addition to cookies and muffins.
- Flax can remain whole in recipes or cracked in a blender or coffee grinder to release additional nutrients.
- Lighter texture in cakes may be achieved by substituting 1 Tbsp (15 mL) freshly ground barley flour for 1 Tbsp (15 mL) freshly ground whole wheat flour.
- Cookie dough may be refrigerated and baked the following day.
- Form cookie dough into a log shape, wrap well, freeze, thaw slightly, slice and bake when desired.
- Add a small amount of water to empty muffin cups before baking muffins to maintain muffin pan quality.
- Cool muffins and cookies in pans, unless otherwise specified, for 5–10 minutes before transferring to wire racks. Cool completely before storing.

- Instant-read thermometers register temperatures quickly.
- Oven thermometers ensure the oven registers the correct temperature.
- Whisks are handy tools to mix dry ingredients evenly.
- You can never own too many timers, whisks, scoops, spatulas, baking pans, or cooling racks!!!

When you have completed a recipe, remember and share with a phone shot. Show your friends. Make something every week!

MAKING DOUGH IN BOSCH UNIVERSAL KITCHEN MACHINES®

Who can resist the smell and taste of homemade bread? Your house smells amazing! After removing bread from the oven, the immediate desire is to promptly cut the hot bread, smother it with butter and devour! I know you want to do this with *all* breads, but there is an exception: breads made with whole grains, seeds and lower gluten flours, such as rye, should be cooled before cutting or they will be gummy and taste unbaked.

Dough made by the following method will be soft and slightly tacky, losing tackiness during the kneading and rising process (developing the gluten). Adding too much flour can result in dry, heavy (dense) bread.

When using fresh milled flour *and* a Bosch Universal Kitchen Machine®, equipped with dough hook, the kneaded dough may be shaped immediately, risen and baked, therefore eliminating several risings, although you may prefer to rise and punch dough more than once before shaping. The higher the protein level of the wheat, the faster gluten develops when kneading, and the faster the bread will rise.

Why knead dough in a Bosch Universal Kitchen Machine®?

- The machines are strong, requiring less kneading time
- The dough will have a shorter rising time
- The machines are efficient and easy to use
- Kneading is less labour-intensive
- The machines are easy to clean
- Less flour is required
- It is convenient

PROCEDURE

Read recipe, gather ingredients and follow these simple instructions:

1. Heat liquids according to recipe and pour into Bosch Universal Kitchen Machine® bowl equipped with dough hook.
2. Add ingredients, except yeast and half the flour.

3. Place splash ring on mixing bowl and pulse or jog momentary switch to incorporate ingredients. Dough will appear as a wet batter.
4. With splash ring in place, add approximately ½ cup (125 mL) flour and the yeast.
5. Turn to speed #1 and add whole grain flour, bread flour or unbleached flour in a constant stream, pouring between the column and inner side of the bowl. When correct amount of flour has been added to the dough (keep reading), remove splash ring and continue kneading on speed #1 to form an elastic, soft ball of dough. Entire amount of flour in the recipe may not be required. The Bosch Universal Kitchen Machine® will knead dough from start to finish with no hand-kneading required.

Dough may be risen in the Bosch Universal Kitchen Machine® with the lid and splash ring in the unlocked position when the bowl is half or less than half full. Allow dough to rise until double in volume. Pulse momentary switch to *punch down* dough to release the air. When the dough amount is more than half of the BOSCH™ bowl, and a rising is desired, remove dough to a large greased bowl, turn the dough over to grease the top, cover and rise to double in volume. Shape, place in prepared pans, rise and bake.

HOW MUCH FLOUR TO ADD?

Using Whole Grain Flour: On speed #1 and splash ring in place, pour flour into the Bosch Universal Kitchen Machine® over liquids, until dough begins to pull away from the *bottom* of the bowl. While dough will appear very moist, don't worry! Bran and germ in whole grain flour will absorb some liquid during kneading and the final product will not be wet.

Knead 7–10 minutes to develop an elastic, stretchy dough. Turn the appliance off at 7 minutes and test elasticity:

- Spread cooking oil on your fingertips
- Remove golf ball size of dough
- Flatten dough into a square or circle and stretch to make a *window,* until light passes through without tearing. If dough tears, return it to the bowl and continue kneading 1–2 minutes. Test elasticity again before shaping.
- Do not over-knead

When dough is stretchy, the gluten is developed and will rise evenly. Divide, shape and place dough into prepared pans or lightly floured brotforms or bannetons (proofing baskets) and rise until double in volume. As dough proofs, the gluten relaxes and is supported by the sides of the pans or brotform. After rising in bannetons, gently invert onto a cornmeal-sprinkled baking sheet, pizza stone or cast-iron casserole dish, and bake as instructed. Brush excess flour from the banneton to store.

Using Bread Flour (High-Gluten Flour) or Unbleached Flour: On speed#1 and splash ring in place, pour flour over liquids into the Bosch Universal Kitchen Machine® equipped with dough hook until dough begins to pull away from the side of the bowl. Knead 4–5 minutes to develop an elastic, stretchy, soft ball of dough. Let dough rise until double in volume, punch down to release air, form into desired shapes, place in prepared pans, rise again and bake as instructed.

BOWL CAPACITY

The Bosch Universal Plus Kitchen Machine® (4-speed) has a 6 ½ litre (6.86 US quarts) bowl capacity and power to knead up to 15 pounds (6.8 kg) of dough, which is about 8 cups (2 L) liquid and 18 cups (4500 mL) of dry ingredients. The 3-speed Bosch Universal Kitchen Machine® can knead up to 12 pounds (5.4 kg) of dough. Alternatively, one loaf of bread or a small amount of pizza dough can be successfully kneaded in either mixer.

KNEADING SMALL QUANTITIES

When small amounts of dough are required, pour all ingredients, except flour and yeast, into the Bosch Universal Kitchen Machine® equipped with dough hook. Place splash ring on the bowl, turn to speed #1, add yeast and gradually pour a constant stream of flour into the bowl until a soft dough ball is formed. Continue as instructed in recipe.

AVOID OVER-KNEADING

German-engineered Bosch Universal Kitchen Machines® are powerful and the dough hook is designed for bread making! Yes—dough can easily be over-kneaded in this strong machine when kneaded for too long, therefore weakening the gluten. Set a timer to check the gluten development (elasticity) before this occurs.

EASY SHAPING - LOAVES

Spread a thin layer of cooking oil on your fingers and work surface to prevent dough from sticking.

Divide dough into desired portions. Flatten one portion at a time on the work surface with your hands to smooth underside of the dough. Gently roll dough from one end, jelly-roll style, to form a log shape the length of the pan. Keeping your thumbs from indenting the dough, the top of the loaf will remain smooth. Lift each roll into prepared pan. Continue with remaining dough, let rise until double in height, and bake as instructed.

Free-form loaves do not require pans. Shape as a loaf or shape as a round loaf by tucking edges and sides underneath the log while turning dough in a circular motion on the work surface. Lift onto a baking sheet sprinkled with cornmeal or into a floured rising basket (banneton). Cover, rise to double in height and bake.

EASY SHAPING - BUNS

Grease both palms and inside of first finger and thumb on one hand with cooking oil. Grasp a manageable section of dough and smooth the top by gently stretching the dough. Form a "C" and squeeze a section of dough between the oiled finger and thumb. *Twist off* the *bun*. Place on a greased baking sheet, well-spaced for crusty buns, barely touching for softer buns, leaving space to accommodate rising. Rise until double in volume and bake as instructed. Form buns the same size for even baking.

IS MY BREAD BAKED?

Before removing from the oven at the end of the recommended baking time, whole wheat and white bread can be tapped gently on the top crust. Baked loaves will sound hollow and have a golden crust. When baking is complete, immediately remove from pans and cool on wire racks to avoid loaves sweating in the pan.

Alternatively, use an instant-read thermometer to read the internal temperature of the baked bread. Insert the thermometer into the end of the loaf without touching the thermometer to the pan. Most yeast breads require an internal temperature of at least 185–190°F (85–88°C); however, rye bread requires an internal temperature of 205–210°F (96–99°C). This ensures the bread is fully baked. Bread will be tough and dry when over-baked.

Store cooled bread in food-safe plastic or cloth bags on the counter, in a drawer or in a bread box. Loaves may be frozen whole or sliced before freezing and thawed as required. Small loaves rise, bake, cool, freeze and defrost faster than large loaves. Breads stored in the refrigerator may soon become dry or stale.

MIXING CAKES, COOKIES AND MUFFINS IN BOSCH UNIVERSAL KITCHEN MACHINES®

Baking should not be difficult, scary, or overwhelming, and too many steps may be discouraging. Hopefully these simple instructions will show you that baking can be easy and fun!

Creaming, beating and mixing is accomplished quickly in a Bosch Universal Kitchen Machine®. Wire whips or paddles rotate four times for each single revolution of the whip drive. Centrifugal force enables whips to touch the bottom of the bowl and mix to incorporate all ingredients well. This efficient action provides the capability to whip cream into butter in mere seconds and create tremendous volume out of only one egg white. In my experience, one large egg white will yield 1 ¼–1 ½ cups (310–375 mL) of whipped egg white. Wow!

Choose wire whips, batter whips, cookie paddles or cake paddles relevant to recipe and assemble in the mixing bowl. Overmixing may cause cookies to flatten, cakes to fall, and muffins to be tough and peaked when baked.

PROCEDURE

Read recipe, gather ingredients and follow these instructions:

1. Place fat and sugar in Bosch Universal Kitchen Machine® equipped with wire or batter whips, cookie or cake paddles, and splash ring. Pulse momentary switch two or three times before continuing to cream on speed #1, 2, 3 or 4 to ensure ingredients do not damage whips (brown sugar should be soft). Add eggs, remaining wet ingredients and flavourings. Mix well. An alternate method is to cream fat, sugar, eggs and vanilla at the same time. Try it! It works!!
2. Measure and add all remaining ingredients to creamed mixture. Set splash ring and lid on the bowl. Pulse momentary switch two or three times. Turn to speed #1 and mix to incorporate dry ingredients. Seriously, this only requires 10–20 seconds!!
3. Remove lids. Follow recipe instructions regarding pans, baking and cooling.

MIXING MANUALLY

Read recipe, gather ingredients and follow these simple instructions when a Bosch Universal Kitchen Machine® is not available:

Breads - In an oversized bowl, mix all ingredients with a wooden spoon or dough whisk, except flour and yeast. Add yeast and enough flour until mixture forms a soft dough. When dough is too stiff to mix with the spoon, turn out onto a floured surface. Add more flour to the dough, kneading with the heel of your hand, until an elastic dough is formed.

Grease mixing bowl and place dough back into the bowl. Turn dough once to grease the top and prevent drying. Cover and let rise until double in bulk. With lightly oiled hands, gently punch air out of dough and rise a second time. Again, punch air from the dough, form desired shapes on a lightly floured or oiled work surface and place in prepared pans, or shape free-form to bake on baking sheets or pizza stones. Rise until double and bake as instructed. Making most breads by hand requires additional kneading and a second rise before shaping.

Cakes, Cookies and Muffins - In a large mixing bowl, cream room-temperature fat and sugar with wooden spoon or whisk. Add eggs and beat very well. Add remaining liquid ingredients and flavourings, and mix well.

In a separate bowl, combine flour, salt and leavening agent with a whisk. Add to wet batter and mix to incorporate and eliminate lumps. Add any additional dry ingredients, such as nuts, raisins, etc. to wet ingredients and mix to combine. Do not overmix cake and muffin batters. Fill prepared pans and bake as instructed.

Breads

YEAST BREADS
CRACKERS
PANCAKES
SCONES
QUICK BREADS

UNBELIEVABLE WHOLE WHEAT BREAD

In February 1984, I began my bread making adventure with this 100% whole wheat recipe (no oil, sugar, honey or eggs). Light and delicious!

5 cups	warm water, 115°F (46°C)	1250 mL
¾ cup	whey powder	175 mL
2 Tbsp	liquid lecithin*	30 mL
¼ tsp	vitamin C crystals (powder)**	1 mL
1 Tbsp	salt	15 mL
10–12 cups	whole wheat flour	2500–3000 mL
2 Tbsp	instant yeast	30 mL

Grind 8 cups (2000 mL) hard wheat berries (kernels for bread) on medium texture setting in NutriMill Flour Mill®. Set aside.

Pour all ingredients, except yeast and 6 cups (1500 mL) flour, into Bosch Universal Kitchen Machine® bowl fitted with dough hook and splash ring. Pulse momentary switch to moisten dry ingredients. Add small scoop of flour and the yeast. Turn to speed #1 and pour a constant stream of flour until dough begins to release from the bottom of the bowl. At this point, dough will appear very moist. However, bran and germ in whole grain flour absorb liquid.

Knead 7–10 minutes to form a soft, stretchy dough.

Oil work surface, form into loaves and place in greased 8 ½ x 4 ½ x 3-inch (21 x 11 x 8 cm) pans. Let rise until double in volume in a warm oven, or cover and rise on the countertop.

Bake 30–35 minutes in a preheated 350°F (180°C) oven until golden brown and loaves sound hollow when tapped.

Transfer baked loaves from pans to wire rack. Cool completely before storing.

*To measure liquid lecithin: pour into mixing bowl and cut off jar edge with a table knife. Wipe knife with paper towel. Lecithin is very sticky and does not rinse well from a cloth.

**Powdered vitamin C may reduce heartburn when warm bread products are consumed.

Yield: 4 loaves

In a warm kitchen, bread from "grain to table" is possible in 1 hour and 7 minutes, using fresh milled flour and Bosch Universal Kitchen Machines®. Even if your finished product takes 1 ½ to 2 hours, I am so proud of you!

Unbelievable Whole Wheat Bread

VARIATIONS FOR UNBELIEVABLE WHOLE WHEAT BREAD

Having fun playing in the kitchen, in February 1984, many variations evolved from my basic whole wheat bread recipe.

CHEESE BREAD

Add 2 cups (500 mL) small cubes cheddar cheese to basic recipe before entire amount of flour is incorporated. Proceed with recipe. Cube cheese with Bosch Universal Kitchen Machine® slicer/shredder French-fry blade.

CRACKED WHEAT BREAD

Crack 1 cup (250 mL) wheat kernels in the blender for 15 seconds, pour into empty mixing bowl and proceed with recipe.

FRENCH ONION BREAD

1 cup	dry onion flakes	250 mL
1 cup	parmesan cheese	250 mL
3 Tbsp	poppy seeds (optional)	45 mL
2 tsp	garlic powder	10 mL
3 Tbsp	powdered beef soup base	45 mL
2 tsp	oregano	10 mL

Add with the 6 cups (1500 mL) flour and continue with instructions. Score tops of loaves with a bread lame (baker's blade) and rise until double in volume.

MULTIGRAIN BREAD

Soak 2 cups (500 mL) whole or cracked grains (wheat, rye, flax, barley, millet, triticale, buckwheat, rice) overnight or several hours in 3–4 cups (750–1000 mL) water. Drain water and pour grains into empty mixing bowl. Proceed with recipe.

VARIATIONS FOR UNBELIEVABLE WHOLE WHEAT BREAD (Continued..)

In February 1984, many more variations evolved from my basic whole wheat bread recipe.

RAISIN BREAD

2 cups	raisins	500 mL	
1 Tbsp	cinnamon	15 mL	

Add during kneading.

RYE BREAD

Follow basic recipe, adding only 7–8 cups (1750–2000 mL) whole wheat flour. Dough will appear very moist and soft. With splash ring on the bowl, knead 5–7 minutes to develop gluten in the whole wheat flour. Slowly add whole grain rye flour, approximately 3-4 cups (750-1000 mL), until dough releases from the side of the bowl.

Continue kneading 2–3 minutes. Rye flour does not require kneading 7–10 minutes.

Shape and place in greased pans. Rise until double in volume. Bake as in *Unbelievable Whole Wheat Bread.*

Decrease whole wheat flour and increase rye flour, according to desired taste.

SEED BREAD

Add 1–2 cups (250–500 mL) mixed seeds to recipe: sesame, pumpkin, sunflower, poppy and flax.

SPROUTED GRAIN BREAD

Pour 2 cups (500 mL) fresh sprouted grains into blender with 2 cups (500 mL) of the 5 cups (1250 mL) water required in recipe. Blend 10 seconds to chop.

Pour into mixing bowl and proceed as in *Unbelievable Whole Wheat Bread.*

Store breads on the counter, in a drawer or bread box, in food-safe plastic bags, linen bags or wrapped in linen towels. Bread products become dry when refrigerated.

BASIC WHITE BREAD

Simple ingredients to make bread in my first year of university, 1975.

4 cups	warm water, 115°F (46°C)	1000 mL
1	egg	1
½ cup	vegetable oil*	125 mL
½ cup	granulated sugar	125 mL
1 Tbsp	salt	15 mL
2 Tbsp	instant yeast	30 mL
10–12 cups	bread or unbleached flour	2500–3000 mL

Pour water, egg, oil, sugar, salt and half the flour into Bosch Universal Kitchen Machine® bowl fitted with dough hook and splash ring. Pulse momentary switch to incorporate flour. Add small scoop of flour and the yeast. On speed #1, gradually add a constant stream of flour until dough begins to pull away from the side of the bowl. Remove splash ring. Knead 4–5 minutes.

Cover bowl with splash ring and lid. Rise dough 15 minutes. Gently deflate dough by pulsing the momentary switch. Cover and rise another 15 minutes. Deflate air from dough. Shape loaves on oiled surface and place in greased 8 ½ x 4 ½ x 3-inch (21 x 11 x 8 cm) pans. Rise until double in volume.

Bake in preheated 350°F (180°C) oven 30 minutes until golden brown.

Transfer baked loaves from pans to wire rack. Cool completely before storing.

Note: Place splash ring in unlocked position when rising dough in the Bosch Universal Kitchen Machine®.

*Exchange melted butter for oil.

Hint: Add ½ cup (125 mL) potato flour for a softer dough.

Yield: 4

CHEESE HERB SLAB

This recipe was developed to demonstrate fun bread treats on the Farm and Ranch Show Culinary Stage, Edmonton, Alberta, 1988.

Knead *Unbelievable Whole Wheat Bread* or *Basic White Bread*. Continue:

Grease pizza pan or large baking sheet.

With lightly oiled hands, spread a thin layer of dough in pan.

Sauté 1 large chopped onion in 2 Tbsp (30 mL) butter and spread on dough. Sprinkle ½ cup (125 mL) chopped sun-dried tomato pieces, marinated in oil and basil, over onions. Sprinkle with basil.

In a small bowl, mix 1 beaten egg into 1 ½ cups (375 mL) shredded cheddar cheese. Spread on dough and sprinkle with poppy seeds.

Rise 10–15 minutes.

Bake in preheated 375°F (190°C) oven 20 minutes. Cut into wedges or slices.

Delicious! Serve hot, warm or cold.

PULL-APARTS

A fun treat using my basic recipe from 1984.

Knead *Unbelievable Whole Wheat Bread* or *Basic White Bread*. Continue:

Prepare Bundt pan: grease well, pour ¼ cup (60 mL) melted butter and ¼ cup (60 mL) pure maple syrup in the pan.

Melt ½ cup (125 mL) butter in a small bowl. In separate bowl, mix 1 cup (250 mL) brown sugar and 2 tsp (10 mL) cinnamon.

With lightly oiled hands, form small buns. Roll each bun in melted butter. Roll in sugar mixture.

Place a layer of buns in prepared pan, leaving space for rising. Stagger second layer of buns between first layer. Follow with third layer.

Rise 30 minutes or until double in volume.

Bake in preheated 350°F (180°C) oven 25–30 minutes.

Pull buns apart and enjoy!

Pull-Aparts

TRITICALE HONEY BREAD

Playing with triticale flour, I created this sweet tasting bread, 1984.

5 cups	warm potato water*, 115°F (46°C)	1250 mL
1 cup	warm water, 115°F (46°C)	250 mL
1 cup	honey	250 mL
⅓ cup	vegetable oil	75 mL
1 cup	nonfat dry milk	250 mL
½ cup	gluten flour	125 mL
2 Tbsp	salt	30 mL
7–8 cups	triticale flour	1750–2000 mL
4 Tbsp	instant yeast	60 mL
5–6 cups	bread or unbleached flour	1250–1500 mL

Pour first 8 ingredients into Bosch Universal Kitchen Machine® bowl fitted with dough hook. Place splash ring on bowl and pulse momentary switch to moisten ingredients. Add small scoop of flour and the yeast. On speed #1, mix for 4 minutes.

Gradually add a constant stream of bread or unbleached flour until dough pulls away from the side of the bowl.

Knead 4–5 minutes.

Place dough in large greased bowl, cover and rise in a warm place until double in volume. Gently deflate air from dough. On oiled surface, shape loaves and place in greased 8 ½ x 4 ½ x 3-inch (21 x 11 x 8 cm) pans.

Rise 30–45 minutes until double in volume.

Bake in preheated 375°F (190°C) oven 45 minutes. Transfer baked loaves from pans to wire rack. While loaves are hot, brush tops with butter for a softer crust.

Cool completely on wire racks before storing.

Yield: 4–5

QUICK AND EASY BUNS

It's easy to pick up a bag of rolls at the supermarket, but if you make my friend Elizabeth's Quick and Easy Buns for your next dinner party, your guests will thank you and remember. She gave me this recipe when I went to university in 1975.

3 cups	warm water, 115°F (46°C)	750 mL
6 Tbsp	vegetable oil	90 mL
2	eggs	2
½ cup	granulated sugar	125 mL
1 tsp	salt	5 mL
2 Tbsp	instant yeast	30 mL
7–9 cups	unbleached flour	1750–2250 mL

Mix water, oil, eggs and sugar in Bosch Universal Kitchen Machine® bowl fitted with dough hook. Add salt, 3 ½ cups (875 mL) flour and the yeast. With splash ring in place, pulse momentary switch to moisten flour. Add more flour in a constant stream until dough releases from the side of the bowl.

Knead 4–5 minutes on speed #1. Rise 15 minutes in the bowl. Pulse momentary switch to gently deflate dough.

Form into buns and place on greased baking sheets, leaving space for rising. Cover and rise one hour or until double in volume.

Bake in preheated 350°F (180°C) oven 15–18 minutes until golden brown and buns sound hollow when tapped.

Transfer baked buns from pans to wire rack. Cool completely before storing.

Yield: 36

*Baking . . . a stress reliever and
an accomplishment!*

PUMPERNICKEL BREAD

Adapted in 1984, I love the flavour and texture of this bread.

3 ½ cups	warm water, 115°F (46°C)	875 mL
½ cup	blackstrap molasses or honey	125 mL
1 Tbsp	vegetable oil	15 mL
2 Tbsp	salt	30 mL
2 cups	cooked, mashed potatoes	500 mL
¾ cup	cornmeal	175 mL
2 tsp	caraway seeds	10 mL
½ cup	sunflower seeds	125 mL
2 Tbsp	carob powder	30 mL
9–10 cups	fresh ground whole wheat flour	2250–2500 mL
4 Tbsp	yeast	60 mL
3 cups	fresh ground rye flour*	750 mL

Grind 7 cups (1750 mL) hard wheat berries (kernels for bread) on medium texture setting in NutriMill Flour Mill®. Set aside.

Grind 2 cups (500 mL) rye berries (kernels) on medium texture setting. Set aside.

Pour first nine ingredients and 4 cups whole wheat flour into Bosch Universal Kitchen Machine® bowl fitted with dough hook and splash ring. Pulse momentary switch to moisten flour. Add ½ cup (125 mL) whole wheat flour and the yeast. Mix gently.

Turn to speed #1, add remaining whole wheat flour. Leaving splash ring in place, knead 5–7 minutes. Dough will appear batter-like. With mixer on speed #1, add a constant stream of rye flour until dough begins to pull away from the side of the bowl. Continue kneading 2-3 minutes.

Oil hands, free-form loaves and place on large baking sheets, or stone sprinkled with cornmeal, and rise until double. Placing loaves at opposite ends of baking sheets allows for rising.

Bake 50 minutes in preheated 350°F (180°C) oven until internal temperature registers 205–210°F (95-100°C) on instant-read thermometer.

Transfer baked loaves to wire rack. Cool completely before slicing or storing.

*Rye flour has a lower gluten content than wheat flour, requiring less kneading.

Yield: 4

COUNTRY FIVE-GRAIN BREAD

I developed this recipe in 1990 for flavour, fibre and texture.

Sponge:

2 cups	warm water, 110–115°F (43–46°C)	500 mL
2 Tbsp	brown sugar	30 mL
1 ½ Tbsp	yeast	22 mL
⅓ cup	rye flour	75 mL
1 ½ cups	whole wheat flour	375 mL

In large bowl, mix sponge ingredients until smooth, about 30 seconds. Cover and let stand at room temperature for an hour until bubbly.

⅓ cup	cornmeal	75 mL
⅓ cup	wheat bran	75 mL
⅓ cup	large flake rolled oats	75 mL
⅓ cup	barley flakes	75 mL
1 Tbsp	salt	15 mL
2 cups	boiling water	500 mL
3 Tbsp	butter or oil	45 mL
6–7 cups	bread flour	1500–1750 mL

Pour cornmeal, wheat bran, rolled oats, barley flakes and salt into Bosch Universal Kitchen Machine® bowl fitted with dough hook and splash ring. Add boiling water and butter or oil.

Mix to moisten and cover bowl. Let stand 15–20 minutes to absorb water and soften grains.

Pour sponge mixture into grain mixture. Place splash ring on mixing bowl.

Turn to speed #1, add flour until dough begins to pull away from the side of the bowl. Knead 4 minutes.

With lightly oiled hands, form four round loaves on oiled surface. Place loaves at opposite ends on two large baking sheets sprinkled with cornmeal. Score tops of loaves with a bread lame (baker's blade). Rise until double in volume.

Bake in preheated 350°F (180°C) oven 30–35 minutes.

Transfer baked loaves from pans to wire rack. Cool completely before slicing or storing.

Yield: 4

BLACK RUSSIAN RYE BREAD

Adapted in 1984, this is one of my favourite breads to bake. Great flavour and texture.

2 ½ cups	warm water, 115°F (46°C)	625 mL
¼ cup	vinegar	60 mL
½ cup	blackstrap molasses	125 mL
¼ cup	carob powder	60 mL
½ cup	butter, melted	125 mL
1 Tbsp	salt	15 mL
2 tsp	instant espresso granules	10 mL
2 Tbsp	dehydrated onion flakes	30 mL
¼ cup	caraway seeds, crushed	60 mL
½ tsp	fennel seeds, crushed	2 mL
2 Tbsp	yeast	30 mL
4–5 cups	fresh ground whole wheat flour	1000–1250 mL
4 cups	fresh ground rye flour	1000 mL
½ cup	cold water	125 mL
1 tsp	cornstarch	5 mL

Cornmeal for dusting

Combine all ingredients except rye flour in Bosch Universal Kitchen Machine® bowl fitted with dough hook and splash ring. Knead 6–7 minutes on speed #1 to develop gluten in wheat flour. Add rye flour until dough begins to pull away from the side of the bowl. Remove splash ring and continue kneading 2–3 minutes.

Grease baking sheet and sprinkle with cornmeal. Oil work surface and shape dough into two round loaves. Place one loaf at each end of a large baking sheet.

Score tops of loaves with a bread lame (baker's blade). Cover loosely with plastic wrap or linen towel and rise until double in volume.

Bake in preheated 350°F (180°C) oven 45–50 minutes until internal temperature registers 205-210°F (95–100°C) on an instant-read thermometer.

Black Russian Rye Bread

While bread is baking, combine cold water and cornstarch in small saucepan. Cook until thick on medium heat. At 45 minutes, remove bread from oven and quickly brush with cornstarch mixture. Return loaves to oven and continue baking 2–3 minutes to set glaze to create a chewy crust.

Transfer baked loaves from pans to wire rack. Cool completely before slicing or storing.

Yield: 2

Black Russian Rye Bread

EZEKIEL BREAD

Adapted in 1984, it is fun to make this unique bread. So nutritious!

6 cups	warm water, 115°F (46°C)	1500 mL
½ cup	butter, melted	125 mL
½ cup	blackstrap molasses or honey	125 mL
1 ½ Tbsp	salt	22 mL
⅓ cup	millet, whole	75 mL
½ cup	wheat gluten	125 mL
3 cups	hard red spring wheat	750 mL
1 cup	rye kernels	250 mL
1 cup	hulled or pot barley	250 mL
¼ cup	pinto beans	60 mL
¼ cup	soy beans	60 mL
¼ cup	green lentils	60 mL
4 cups	hard red spring wheat*	1000 mL
3 Tbsp	yeast	45 mL

Grind 3 cups (750 mL) wheat, rye, barley, beans and lentils into whole grain flour on coarse texture setting in NutriMill Flour Mill®. Set aside.

Grind 4 cups (1000 mL) hard wheat (kernels for bread) on medium texture setting. Set aside. *Spelt may be exchanged for wheat.

Pour water, butter, molasses, salt, millet, gluten and grain and bean flour into Bosch Universal Kitchen Machine® bowl fitted with dough hook and splash ring. Pulse momentary switch to combine ingredients. Add yeast and turn to speed #1.

Add whole wheat flour from second bowl of flour until dough begins to pull away from the bottom of the bowl. Knead 7–10 minutes.

With lightly oiled hands, shape dough into 4 round loaves on oiled surface. Place loaves on two large baking sheets or two baking stones, each sprinkled with cornmeal.* Score tops of loaves with a bread lame (baker's blade) and rise until double in volume.

Bake 35 minutes in preheated 350°F (180°C) oven. Transfer baked loaves from pans to wire rack. Cool completely before storing.

*Dough may be risen in well-floured bannetons (rising baskets). Proceed as in *Pumpernickel Bread*.

Yield: 4

"Take wheat and barley, beans and lentils, millet and spelt; put them in a storage jar and use them to make bread for yourself."
—Ezekiel 4:9

ANCIENT 14-GRAIN BREAD

I originally met Shar, from Arizona, US, at a BOSCH™ convention in March 1986. We were both BOSCH™ distributors with similar stores. Exchanging recipes, ideas and lots of laughter, we remain very good friends. She gave me this wonderful recipe in 1988.

6 cups	warm water, 115°F (46°C)	1500 mL
2 cups	12-grain bread mix*	500 mL
½ cup	whole grain amaranth	125 mL
½ cup	whole grain quinoa	125 mL
½ cup	teff seeds	125 mL
⅔ cup	canola or vegetable oil	150 mL
⅔ cup	honey	150 mL
3 Tbsp	dough enhancer	45 mL
3 Tbsp	instant yeast	45 mL
2 Tbsp	salt	30 mL
2 cups	spelt flour	500 mL
2 cups	Kamut® flour	500 mL
2 cups	bread flour**	500 mL
9–10 cups	whole wheat flour	2250–2500 mL

Grind 7 cups (1750 mL) hard wheat berries (kernels for bread) on medium texture setting in NutriMill Flour Mill®. Grind spelt and Kamut® kernels, if available. Set aside.

Rinse amaranth, quinoa and teff in a very fine sieve. Pour into Bosch Universal Kitchen Machine® bowl fitted with dough hook. Add remaining ingredients except whole wheat flour. Place splash ring on mixing bowl and pulse momentary switch to combine.

Turn to speed #1 and add whole wheat flour until dough begins to pull away from bottom of the bowl. Remove splash ring and knead 7–10 minutes.

Oil work surface, form into five loaves and place in greased 8 ½ x 4 ½ x 3-inch (21 x 11 x 8 cm) pans.

Cover and rise 50–60 minutes until loaves double in volume.

Bake in preheated 350°F (180°C) oven 30–35 minutes until internal temperature registers 185–190°F (85-90°C) on an instant-read thermometer and loaves are golden brown.

Transfer baked loaves from pans to wire rack. Cool completely before storing.

*Exchange multigrain or 9-grain mix for 12-grain mix.
**Bread flour may be exchanged for whole wheat flour.

Yield: 5

"The joy of the Lord is your strength."
—Nehemiah 8:10

SEVEN-GRAIN BREAD

I created this recipe in 1990.

2 cups	whole wheat kernels	500 mL
1 cup	triticale kernels	250 mL
1 cup	rye kernels	250 mL
1 cup	millet	250 mL
1 cup	barley	250 mL
½ cup	dried yellow corn	125 mL
½ cup	brown rice	125 mL
5 ½ cups	warm water, 115°F (46°C)	1375 mL
⅓ cup	honey	75 mL
⅓ cup	blackstrap molasses	75 mL
1 ½ Tbsp	salt	22 mL
¼ cup	oil or melted butter	60 mL
½ cup	gluten flour	125 mL
2 Tbsp	yeast	30 mL
5-6 cups	bread flour*	1250–1500 mL

Measure all grains and grind into flour on medium texture setting in NutriMill Flour Mill®. Reserve.

Pour water, honey, molasses, salt and oil into Bosch Universal Kitchen Machine® bowl fitted with dough hook. Add reserved flour. Place splash ring on mixing bowl and mix well by pulsing momentary switch. Add gluten and yeast. On speed #1, add bread flour until dough begins to pull away from the side of the bowl. Knead 5–7 minutes. Cover mixing bowl and rise until double in volume.

Gently deflate dough and shape into 5 loaves. Place each loaf in well-greased 8 ½ x 4 ½ x 3-inch (21 x 11 x 8 cm) pan and rise until double in volume.

Bake in preheated 350°F (180°C) oven 30–35 minutes.

Transfer baked loaves from pans to wire rack. Brush with melted butter for a softer crust. Cool completely before slicing or storing.

*Substitute fresh ground whole wheat flour for bread flour and knead 7–10 minutes.

Option: Proof active dry yeast in 2 cups (500 mL) of the water and the honey, about 10 minutes until bubbly.

Yield: 5

FOUR-SEED BREAD

I developed this recipe in 1990 to use seeds from my pantry.

5 cups	warm water 110–115°F (43–46°C)	1250 mL
½ cup	blackstrap molasses	125 mL
½ cup	honey	125 mL
1 Tbsp	malt powder, optional*	15 mL
1 Tbsp	granulated sugar	15 mL
1 Tbsp	salt	15 mL
1 Tbsp	dough enhancer	15 mL
3 Tbsp	yeast	45 mL
2 cups	millet	500 mL
1 ½ cups	sunflower seeds	375 mL
½ cup	sesame seeds	125 mL
½ cup	poppy seeds	125 mL
10–12 cups	whole wheat flour	2500–3000 mL

Grind 8 cups (2000 mL) hard wheat berries (kernels for bread) on medium texture setting in NutriMill Flour Mill®. Set aside.

Mix water, molasses, honey, malt powder, sugar, salt, dough enhancer and yeast in Bosch Universal Kitchen Machine® bowl fitted with dough hook and splash ring. Rest 5 minutes.

Add millet, sunflower, sesame and poppy seeds.

Turn to speed #1, add whole wheat flour until dough begins to pull away from the bottom of the bowl. Knead 7–10 minutes.

With lightly oiled hands, form loaves on oiled surface. Place in greased 8 ½ x 4 ½ x 3-inch (21 x 11 x 8 cm) pans. Rise until double in volume.

Bake in preheated 350°F (180°C) oven 30–35 minutes.

Transfer baked loaves from pans to wire rack. Cool completely before slicing or storing.

*Malt powder is available in specialty food stores.

Yield: 6

BARLEY WHOLE WHEAT BREAD

I created this recipe in 1994. The barley flour adds a bit of sour flavour without a sourdough starter.

5 cups	warm water, 110–115°F (43–46°C)	1250 mL
¼ tsp	vitamin C crystals	1 mL
⅓ cup	oil	75 mL
2 Tbsp	granulated sugar*	30 mL
1 Tbsp	salt	15 mL
3 cups	barley flour	750 mL
3 cups	whole wheat flour	750 mL
2 Tbsp	yeast	30 mL
5–6 cups	bread or unbleached flour	1250–1500 mL

Grind barley grain kernels and hard wheat berries (kernels for bread) on medium texture setting in NutriMill Flour Mill®. Measure flours and set aside.

Pour first 7 ingredients into Bosch Universal Kitchen Machine® bowl fitted with dough hook and splash ring. Pulse momentary switch to moisten flour. Add yeast and knead on speed #1, 4–5 minutes to develop gluten.

Add bread or unbleached flour until dough begins to pull away from the side of the bowl and continue kneading 4–5 minutes.

Allow dough to rise 30 minutes. Gently deflate air from dough. Shape and place in greased 8 ½ x 4 ½ x 3-inch (21 x 11 x 8 cm) pans. Rise until double in volume.

Bake in preheated 350°F (180°C) oven 30 minutes.

Transfer loaves to wire rack. Cool before storing.

*Increase sugar for sweeter dough.

Store remaining barley and wheat flour in freezer.

Yield: 4

OLIVE BREAD

Since I like to eat olives and bread, I combined them in this recipe, 1994.

1 Tbsp	yeast	15 mL
1 Tbsp	granulated sugar	15 mL
¾ cup	warm water, 110–115°F (43–46°C)	175 mL
1 ½ cups	warm milk, 110–115°F (43–46°C)	375 mL
⅓ cup	olive oil	75 mL
1 ½ tsp	salt	7 mL
1 ½ tsp	thyme	7 mL
1 ½ tsp	chili flakes	7 mL
5–6 cups	bread or unbleached flour	1250–1500 mL
1 cup	pimento stuffed green olives, drained, halved	250 mL
2 cups	pitted black olives, drained, halved	500 mL

Cornmeal for dusting

In small bowl, sprinkle sugar and yeast over warm water. Let stand until foamy, about 10 minutes.

Pour milk, oil, salt, thyme, chili flakes, and 2 cups (500 mL) flour into Bosch Universal Kitchen Machine® bowl fitted with dough hook. Fit splash ring on mixing bowl and mix gently with momentary switch. Add yeast mixture.

Turn to speed #1 and add flour until dough begins to pull away from the side of the bowl. Knead 4–5 minutes. Add olives during last few seconds of kneading.

Cover mixing bowl and rise dough until double in volume. Gently deflate dough. With lightly oiled hands, form two round loaves on oiled surface. Place on pizza peel(s) sprinkled with cornmeal. Score tops of loaves with a bread lame (bakers' blade). Rise until double in volume.

Preheat oven to 375°F (190°C). Place oven proof container with 1-inch (2.5 cm) water on lowest rack. Transfer loaves to baking stones* sprinkled with cornmeal.

Bake 40–45 minutes. Transfer baked loaves from stone to wire rack. Cool completely before storing.

*Follow pizza/baking stone directions. Some baking stones require a cool oven.

Alternate baking methods: After first rise, shape and place in greased loaf pans or a floured banneton (rising basket). Rise until double in volume. Gently transfer dough from banneton to large baking sheet or stone sprinkled with cornmeal. Bake.

Yield: 2

TROPICAL BREAD

I met Shar, from Arizona, US, at a BOSCH™ convention in March 1986. We were both BOSCH™ distributors with similar stores. Exchanging recipes, ideas and lots of laughter, we remain very good friends. She gave me this unique recipe in 1988.

5 cups	warm water, 110–115°F (43–46°C)	1250 mL
⅔ cup	vegetable oil	150 mL
⅔ cup	honey	150 mL
2 Tbsp	salt	30 mL
3 Tbsp	dough enhancer	45 mL
3 Tbsp	instant yeast	45 mL
1 Tbsp	vanilla	15 mL
6 cups	whole wheat flour	1500 mL
2 cups	dried cranberries	500 mL
1 cup	dried mangoes, chopped	250 mL
1 cup	dried pineapple, chopped	250 mL
1 cup	dried papaya, chopped	250 mL
1 cup	unsweetened ribbon coconut	250 mL
½ cup	dried apricots, chopped	125 mL
1 cup	macadamia nuts, chopped	250 mL
5–7 cups	bread flour	1250–1750 mL

Combine water, oil, honey, salt, dough enhancer, yeast, vanilla and 5 cups (1250 mL) whole wheat flour in Bosch Universal Kitchen Machine® bowl fitted with dough hook.

In medium-size bowl, stir one cup of whole wheat flour into fruit and nuts, to separate dried fruits. Add fruit mixture. Place splash ring on bowl. Pulse momentary switch to combine ingredients. Turn to speed #1 and knead 4–5 minutes.

Add bread flour until dough begins to pull away from the side of the bowl. Continue kneading 4 minutes.

Cover dough and rise until double in volume. Gently deflate air with the momentary switch. With lightly oiled hands, form into loaves on oiled surface and place in greased 8 ½ x 4 ½ x 3-inch (21 x 11 x 8 cm) pans. Rise until double in volume.

Bake in preheated 350°F (180°C) oven 35–40 minutes until golden brown and internal temperature registers 185–190°F (85-90°C) on instant-read thermometer.

Transfer loaves to wire rack. Cool before slicing or storing.

Yield: 6

FRECKLE BREAD

I met Shar, from Arizona, US, at a BOSCH™ convention in March 1986. We were both BOSCH™ distributors with similar stores. Exchanging recipes, ideas and lots of laughter, we remain very good friends. She gave me this fun recipe in 1988.

4 cups	warm water, 115°F (46°C)	1000 mL
⅔ cup	honey	150 mL
½ cup	vegetable oil	125 mL
3 Tbsp	dough enhancer	45 mL
2 cups	bread flour	500 mL
2 Tbsp	potato flour	30 mL
4	eggs	4
2 cups	carrots, grated	500 mL
1 cup	dried currants	250 mL
1 ½ cups	golden raisins	375 mL
1 cup	dried pineapple, cut into small pieces	250 mL
2 Tbsp	salt	30 mL
4 Tbsp	instant yeast	60 mL
14–16 cups	whole wheat flour	3500–4000 mL

Grind 11 cups (2750 mL) hard wheat berries (kernels for bread) on medium texture setting in NutriMill Flour Mill®. Set aside.

Pour all ingredients except yeast and whole wheat flour into Bosch Universal Kitchen Machine® bowl fitted with dough hook.

Add 5 cups (1250 mL) whole wheat flour, position splash ring and pulse to mix. Add 1 small scoop flour and the yeast. Pulse to moisten.

Turn to speed #1 and add flour until dough begins to pull away from bottom of the bowl. Knead 7–8 minutes until gluten has developed into a stretchy dough.

Shape into large free formed loaves and place on a baking stone sprinkled with cornmeal or place in greased 5 x 10-inch (12.7 x 25.4 cm) loaf pans.

Score tops of bread with a bread lame (baker's blade).

Brush loaves with 1 beaten egg and 1 Tbsp (15 mL) water and rise until double in volume.

Bake in preheated 350°F (180°C) oven 35–40 minutes until internal temperature registers 190-200°F (90-95°C) on instant-read thermometer.

Transfer loaves to wire rack. Cool before slicing.

Yield: 5

COUNTRY MILLET AND CORN BREAD

I met Shar, from Arizona, US, at a BOSCH™ convention in March 1986. We were both BOSCH™ distributors with similar stores. Exchanging recipes, ideas and lots of laughter, we remain very good friends. She gave me this recipe in 1988.

1 ½ cups	uncooked millet	375 mL
2 ¾ cups	boiling water	675 mL
⅓ cup	canola or vegetable oil	75 mL
2 Tbsp	brown sugar	30 mL
2 Tbsp	instant yeast	30 mL
¾ cup	cornmeal	175 mL
1 Tbsp	salt	15 mL
4–5 cups	whole wheat flour	1000–1250 mL
1 ½ cups	bread or unbleached flour	375 mL

Grind 3 cups (750 mL) hard wheat berries (kernels for bread). Set aside.

Soak millet in the water for one hour in Bosch Universal Kitchen Machine® bowl fitted with dough hook and lids.

Add oil, sugar, yeast, cornmeal, salt and whole wheat flour. Knead 4–5 minutes on speed #1.

With mixer on, add flour until dough begins to pull away from the side of the bowl. Knead 4–5 minutes until gluten develops into a stretchy dough.

Oil work surface, shape into loaves and place in greased 8 ½ x 4 ½ x 3-inch (21 x 11 x 8 cm) pans. Score tops of loaves with a bread lame (baker's blade) and allow to rise until double in volume.

Bake in preheated 350°F (180°C) oven 30–40 minutes until internal temperature registers 190–200°F (90–95°C) on instant-read thermometer.

Transfer loaves to wire rack. Cool before storing.

Yield: 2

HOT CROSS BUNS

I enjoy hot cross buns, so I developed this spicy recipe, 1983.

2	whole eggs	2
2	egg yolks	2
2 cups	milk, scald, cool slightly	500 mL
1 cup	warm water	250 mL
1 ⅓ cups	granulated sugar	325 mL
4 tsp	salt	20 mL
⅔ cup	butter	150 mL
¾ tsp	cinnamon	3 mL
1 tsp	nutmeg	5 mL
¾ tsp	mace	3 mL
¾ tsp	ginger	3 mL
1 ⅓ cups	raisins or currants	325 mL
1 cup	mixed peel or candied fruit	250 mL
8–10 cups	bread or unbleached flour	2000–2500 mL
3 Tbsp	instant yeast	45 mL
2	egg whites	2
2 Tbsp	water	30 mL

Pour first 13 ingredients into Bosch Universal Kitchen Machine® bowl fitted with dough hook. Add 3 cups (750 mL) flour and the yeast. Place splash ring on mixing bowl and pulse momentary switch to mix gently.

Turn to speed #1 and add flour until dough begins to pull away from the side of the bowl. Knead 4–5 minutes. Allow dough to rise until double in volume. Gently deflate dough and form into buns. Place buns in greased baking pans. Score a shallow cross on each bun with a bread lame (baker's blade).

Brush buns with 2 lightly beaten egg whites mixed with 2 Tbsp (30 mL) water and rise until double in volume.

Bake in preheated 350°F (180°C) oven 18–20 minutes. Drizzle *Icing Sugar Glaze* in the cross on warm buns.

ICING SUGAR GLAZE

1 Tbsp	milk	15 mL
¾ cup	confectioner's (icing) sugar	175 mL
¼ tsp	vanilla	1 mL

Mix well in a small bowl. Drizzle in cross. Cool on wire rack before storing.

Yield: 48

SOURDOUGH STARTER

2 cups	lukewarm water, 105–110°F (40–43°C)	500 mL
½ tsp	active dry yeast	2 mL
1 Tbsp	granulated sugar	15 mL
¼ cup	buttermilk powder	60 mL
⅓ cup	plain yogurt*	75 mL
2 cups	bread flour	500 mL

Pour warm water in a glass bowl or crock. Sprinkle sugar and yeast on the water. Add remaining ingredients and mix with a wooden spoon or silicone whisk.

Allow starter to ferment 3–5 days, stirring 2–3 times each day. Lumps will break apart as bubbles form and starter ferments. Refrigerate.

To make *Sourdough Bread,* warm starter to room temperature. Feed starter.

*Yogurt quickens fermentation time, but may be omitted.

FEEDING SOURDOUGH STARTER

To feed and retain starter volume, add:

1 cup flour	250 mL
1 cup liquid buttermilk or whole milk*	250 mL

Mix with wooden spoon or silicone whisk. Ferment 2 or 3 days, stirring occasionally.

*Buttermilk or whole milk powder may be used: 3 Tbsp (45 mL) powder to 1 cup (250 mL) water. Measure powder and add water to 1 cup (250 mL) mark on measuring cup. Whisk well.

*Biscuit, pancake and waffle recipes
may require sourdough starter.*

FARMSTEAD SOURDOUGH BREAD

Sourdough bread is one of my favourites, so I created an easy starter and recipe, 1988.

1 ½ cups	warm water, 110–115°F (43–46°C)	375 mL
1 Tbsp	active dry yeast	15 mL
1 Tbsp	granulated sugar	15 mL
1 cup	sourdough starter	250 mL
½ cup	butter, melted	125 mL
1 Tbsp	salt	15 mL
¾ cup	multigrain cereal*	175 mL
5–6 cups	bread or unbleached flour	1250–1500 mL
¼ cup	cornmeal	60 mL
1	egg white, beaten	1
2 Tbsp	multigrain cereal	30 mL

In small bowl, pour ½ cup (125 mL) warm water, one tsp (5 mL) of the sugar, and sprinkle yeast on the water. Stir to dissolve sugar and rest 10 minutes to activate yeast and create bubbles. Proceed as in *Basic White Bread* if using instant yeast.

Pour starter, remaining warm water, sugar, butter, salt and ¾ cup (175 mL) multigrain cereal in Bosch Universal Kitchen Machine® bowl fitted with dough hook and splash ring. Add yeast mixture.

Turn to speed #1 and add flour until dough begins to pull away from the side of the bowl. Remove splash ring and knead 4–5 minutes until dough is smooth and stretchy. Cover dough, let rise about 1 hour until double in volume.

Gently deflate dough with momentary switch. Grease two 8 ½ x 4 ½ x 3-inch (21 x 11 x 8 cm) pans and sprinkle with cornmeal. Shape dough on oiled surface and lift into prepared pans. Score loaves with a bread lame (baker's blade). Brush loaves with beaten egg white and sprinkle with 2 Tbsp (30 mL) multigrain cereal. Cover loaves, let rise for 45–60 minutes until double in volume.

Preheat oven to 350°F (180°C) before dough is completely risen.

Bake 35–40 minutes on centre rack until golden brown and sound hollow when tapped. Transfer baked loaves from pans to wire rack. Cool completely before slicing or storing.

*Multigrain cereal contains: barley flakes, large flake rolled oats, rye flakes, triticale flakes, wheat flakes, spelt flakes, flax seed, and hulled millet.

Yield: 2

ENGLISH MUFFINS

So easy and delicious, we have been enjoying this recipe since 1984.

1 ⅓ cups	warm water, 110–115°F (43–46°C)	325 mL
2 Tbsp	honey or blackstrap molasses	30 mL
⅓ cup	canola or vegetable oil	75 mL
2	eggs	2
1 ½ tsp	salt	7 mL
2 Tbsp	instant yeast	30 mL
3–4 cups	whole wheat flour*	750–1000 mL
	cornmeal	

Grind 3 cups (750 mL) hard wheat berries (kernels) on medium texture setting in NutriMill Flour Mill®. Set aside.

Pour water, honey or molasses, oil, eggs and salt in Bosch Universal Kitchen Machine® bowl fitted with dough hook and splash ring. Pulse momentary switch to mix gently. Add yeast and pour a constant stream of flour until dough begins to pull away from bottom of the bowl. Knead 7–10 minutes. Cover dough and rise until double in volume.

Roll dough on a lightly oiled surface to ½-inch (1.3 cm) thickness. Cut out muffins with a 3-inch (7.6 cm) biscuit cutter.

Dip both sides of dough circles in cornmeal and cook on a lightly greased 275°F (140°C) griddle 8–10 minutes on each side, turning once.

Cool on wire racks before storing.

Recipe doubles well.

*Substitute bread flour for whole wheat flour. Knead 4–5 minutes.

Yield: 12

BABKA (UKRAINIAN EASTER SWEET BREAD)

Adapted in 1988, this recipe is a favourite in our home.

6	egg yolks	6
4	eggs	4
1 cup	granulated sugar	250 mL
½ cup	lukewarm water	125 mL
¾ cup	butter, melted	175 mL
2 cups	milk, scald, cool slightly	500 mL
1 tsp	salt	5 mL
1 tsp	vanilla	5 mL
2	oranges	2
9–10 cups	bread or unbleached flour	2250–2500 mL
2 Tbsp	yeast	30 mL
1 cup	raisins	250 mL

Scald milk, wash and dry raisins, melt butter, zest and juice 2 oranges.

Mix eggs and sugar in Bosch Universal Kitchen Machine® bowl fitted with dough hook. Add water, butter, milk, salt, vanilla, rind, juice, raisins, 4 cups (1000 mL) flour and yeast. Place splash ring in position and pulse momentary switch.

Turn to speed #1 and add 5–6 cups (1250-1500 mL) flour until dough releases from the side of the bowl.

Knead 4–5 minutes and rise until double in volume. Gently deflate dough, shape and place in greased panettone molds, deep springform pans or souffle dishes. Rise again until double in volume.

Bake in preheated 325°F (165°C) oven about 1 hour until golden brown and firm to touch.

Transfer baked loaves from pans to wire rack. Cool completely before storing.

Yield: 4

Faith makes you strong!

PANETTONE BREAD

Citron, raisins and pinenuts go together so well that I adapted this recipe in 1990. Regularly served in our home, our children called it 'mushroom' bread because of the shape.

3 ½ cups	milk, scald, cool slightly	875 mL
2 cups	citron peel	500 mL
1 cup	dark raisins	250 mL
1 cup	golden or sultana raisins	250 mL
1 cup	nuts or pine nuts, toasted*	250 mL
3	eggs	3
¼ cup	butter, melted	60 mL
½ tsp	cardamom	2 mL
1 Tbsp	salt	15 mL
1 ½ tsp	pure vanilla (optional)	7 mL
8–9 cups	bread flour**	2000–2250 mL
2 Tbsp	yeast	30 mL

Scald milk and cool slightly to 120°F (49°C). Pour milk into Bosch Universal Kitchen Machine® bowl fitted with dough hook, add butter, 4 cups (1000 mL) flour, fruit, nuts, eggs, salt and flavouring.

Place splash ring on mixing bowl and pulse momentary switch to moisten ingredients. Add yeast, turn to speed #1. Add flour in a constant stream until dough begins to pull away from the side of the mixing bowl.

Knead 4–5 minutes. Rise until double in volume.

Shape into two large loaves 10 x 5 x 3-inch (25 x 13 x 8 cm) or place round shaped balls in greased soufflé dishes or deep springform pans. Rise until double in volume.

Bake 45 minutes in a preheated 350°F (180°C) oven. Transfer baked loaves from pans to wire rack. Cool completely before storing.

*Toast nuts in an ungreased skillet, on medium heat, until golden and aromatic. Pour on plate or cutting board to cool.

**Substitute fresh ground whole wheat flour for bread flour. Add flour until dough begins to pull away from the bottom of the bowl. Knead 7–10 minutes.

Option: Shape into two large round loaves and place on large baking sheet sprinkled with cornmeal or shape and rise in well-floured bannetons. Gently transfer onto a baking sheet when double in volume. Bake.

Panettone, an Italian sweet bread, is often prepared for Christmas and New Year's but is delicious any time of the year!

Panettone Bread

WHOLE WHEAT PIZZA DOUGH

2 cups	warm water, 110–115°F (43–46°C)	500 mL
2 tsp	honey	10 mL
2 tsp	yeast	10 mL
1 Tbsp	olive oil	15 mL
½ tsp	salt	2 mL
⅔ cup	whole wheat flour	150 mL
3 ½ cups	unbleached flour	875 mL

Pour first 6 ingredients into Bosch Universal Kitchen Machine® bowl fitted with dough hook and splash ring. Turn to speed #1 and add unbleached flour until dough releases from the side of the bowl.

Knead 4–5 minutes. Let dough rise until double in volume.

Turn dough onto a lightly floured surface. Roll to desired thickness and size. Assemble pizza as in *Pizza Dough* recipe.

Option: Cover dough and refrigerate up to 2 days.

Yield: 3

ITALIAN PIZZA DOUGH

This recipe is from Barb's Culinary Tour of Italy 2015.

1 Kg	00 pizza flour
50 g	olive oil
15 g	salt
20 g	yeast
	warm water

In medium-size mixing bowl, pour flour, oil, salt and yeast. Add warm water to pull dough together and make a soft dough. Knead gently a few minutes. Let dough rest and rise.

Divide dough into balls. Flatten each ball on a lightly floured surface.

Prepare sauce and toppings for pizza. Drizzle with olive oil.

Bake 5–6 minutes at 200–220°C (390–430°F) on a hot baking stone sprinkled with cornmeal.

Ingredients in European recipes are measured by weight.

PIZZA DOUGH

I created this easy recipe in 1972. Multiply the recipe according to your appetite and family size.

½ cup	lukewarm water	125 mL
½ tsp	granulated sugar	2 mL
½ tsp	yeast	2 mL
½ tsp	salt	2 mL
2 Tbsp	olive oil	30 mL
1 ¼ cups	unbleached flour*	310 mL

Using active dry yeast, stir sugar into warm water and sprinkle with yeast. Activate yeast for 5–10 minutes to form bubbles. Continue with recipe. Instant yeast does not require proofing, but may be proofed if desired.

Pour yeast mixture and oil into Bosch Universal Kitchen Machine® bowl fitted with dough hook and splash ring. Turn to speed #1, add remaining ingredients. Knead 3–4 minutes to form a smooth, stretchy dough.

Turn dough onto a lightly floured surface. Roll dough to a thin, 16-18-inch (40-45 cm) diameter circle and place on a baking stone sprinkled with cornmeal, or in a greased baking or pizza pan. Spread a thin layer of olive oil on dough with a pastry brush. Spread a thin layer of pizza sauce on dough. Top with desired toppings.

Bake at 375–400°F (190–200°C) 15–20 minutes until crust is golden brown.

*Exchange with 00 pizza flour (extra fine flour for pizza).

Yield: 1

SEMOLINA PIZZA DOUGH

2 cups	warm water, 110–115°F (43–46°C)	500 mL
1 tsp	honey	5 mL
2 tsp	yeast	10 mL
1 Tbsp	olive oil	15 mL
½ tsp	salt	2 mL
2 cups	semolina flour	500 mL
2 ⅓ cups	unbleached flour	575 mL

Follow *Pizza Dough* recipe instructions.

Yield: 3

CHEESE CRACKERS

Fun to make, I adapted this recipe in 1984, after buying a flour mill.

⅓ cup	milk	75 mL
1 Tbsp	vinegar	15 mL
1 ¼ cups	whole wheat flour	310 mL
¼ tsp	baking soda	1 mL
½ cup	wheat germ	125 mL
½ cup	butter	125 mL
½ cup	sharp cheddar cheese, grated	125 mL

Preheat oven to 375°F (190°C).

Grind 1 cup (250 mL) wheat kernels on medium texture setting in NutriMill Flour Mill®. Set aside.

In small bowl, combine milk and vinegar. Set aside.

Combine flour, baking soda, wheat germ, butter and cheese in Bosch Universal Kitchen Machine® bowl fitted with dough hook and splash ring. Mix to resemble coarse meal. Add milk mixture and mix to incorporate. Knead briefly.

On lightly floured surface, roll dough to 1/4-inch (6.5 mm) thick, and cut into 2 x 1-inch (5 x 2.5 cm) rectangles.

Place on baking sheet and gently poke holes, using a fork or docker, evenly on each cracker.

Option: Add ¼ tsp (1 mL) cayenne pepper to dry ingredients.

Bake 15 minutes.

Cool before storing.

Yield: 60

BLENDER PANCAKES

I have been making these pancakes often since 1984. Flavour, fibre and texture!

| 1 cup | milk | 250 mL |
| ¾ cup | whole wheat kernels (berries) | 175 mL |

Pour milk and wheat into a blender. Blend 4 minutes.

Add and mix for 10 seconds:

2	eggs	2
2 Tbsp	granulated sugar or honey	30 mL
¾ tsp	baking soda	3 mL
½ tsp	salt	2 mL
¼ cup	vegetable oil	60 mL
2 Tbsp	baking powder	30 mL

Pour blended batter onto hot, greased griddle, to desired size, and cook until golden brown. Flip once when bubbles form on pancakes.

Pancakes of equal diameters cook evenly.

Serve with desired toppings: butter, syrup, jam, peanut butter, chocolate, fruit, whipped cream, etc.

Pancakes freeze well.

Reheat in a toaster.

BUTTERMILK PANCAKE MIX

Adapted in 1984.

8 cups	whole wheat flour	2000 mL
1 cup	soy flour	250 mL
1 cup	buckwheat flour	250 mL
1 cup	millet flour	250 mL
1 cup	rye flour	250 mL
1 cup	corn flour	250 mL
1 cup	oat flour	250 mL
1 cup	barley flour	250 mL
1 cup	triticale flour	250 mL
4 cups	buttermilk powder	1000 mL
3 Tbsp	salt	45 mL
¼ cup	baking soda	60 mL

Combine all ingredients well and store in a covered container in the freezer.

Note: Grind fresh flour from grains for best flavour. Substitute flours as desired.

BUTTERMILK PANCAKES

2 ½ cups	*Buttermilk Pancake Mix*	625 mL
2 cups	water	500 mL
2	eggs, beaten	2
¼ cup	canola or vegetable oil	60 mL

Combine *Buttermilk Pancake Mix* and water. Add beaten eggs and oil. Mix only until blended.

Pour onto a lightly greased 375°F (190°C) griddle and bake until bubbly and golden brown. Turn once.

Yield: 20, 4-inch (10 cm) pancakes

Keep mix ready for healthy, flavourful,
easy pancakes anytime.

CHERRY SCONES

I enjoy scones and cherries so much, in 1992 I developed a recipe just for me (but I'll share it with you).

3–4 cups	whole wheat flour*	750–1000 mL
2 Tbsp	granulated sugar	30 mL
1 Tbsp	baking powder	15 mL
½ tsp	salt	2 mL
½ tsp	cream of tartar	2 mL
½ cup	butter, room temperature	125 mL
1	egg, separated	1
½ cup	sour cream	125 mL
¾ cup	half and half cream	175 mL
1 ½ tsp	almond extract	7 mL
¾ cup	dried cherries**	175 mL
	coarse sugar	

Preheat oven to 400°F (200°C).

Combine flour, sugar, baking powder, salt and cream of tartar in Bosch Universal Kitchen Machine® bowl fitted with wire whips and splash ring. Cut butter into dry ingredients by pulsing the momentary switch until mixture resembles coarse crumbs. Replace dough hook for wire whips or use cookie paddles for the entire recipe.

Add egg yolk, sour cream, cream, extract and cherries to flour mixture and mix briefly to form a soft dough.

Gently knead dough on a lightly floured surface. Divide dough in half and shape into balls.

Pat each portion into an 8-inch (20 cm) circle and score into six wedges with a pizza cutter or bench scraper. Place 1-inch (2.5 cm) apart on ungreased baking sheet.

Beat reserved egg white until foamy. Brush tops with egg white and sprinkle with coarse sugar.

Bake 15–20 minutes until golden brown. Serve warm. Cool before storing.

*Remove bran and germ from whole grain flour for a lighter texture.

**If cherries are extremely dry, soak in boiling water 10 minutes. Drain well.

Yield: 12

CHOCOLATE SCONES

2 ½ cups	unbleached flour	625 mL
2 Tbsp	granulated sugar	30 mL
4 tsp	baking powder	20 mL
¼ tsp	salt	1 mL
⅓ cup	cold unsalted butter, cubed	75 mL
¾ cup	whipping cream*	175 mL
2	eggs	2
1 tsp	pure vanilla	5 mL
1 cup	pure semi-sweet chocolate chips	250 mL
1	egg yolk	1
1 tsp	water	5 mL

Preheat oven to 450°F (230°C).

In small bowl, whisk cream, eggs and vanilla together.

In large bowl, stir flour, sugar, baking powder and salt. Use a pastry blender to cut butter into flour mixture to the size of small peas or coarse crumbs. Stir cream mixture into dry ingredients with a fork to form a dough. Stir in chocolate.

Turn dough onto a lightly floured surface. Knead once or twice with the heal of your hand until dough comes together.

Roll or pat dough into a 9-inch (23 cm) square. Cut into 9 squares. Cut each square in half diagonally and place triangles 1-inch (2.5 cm) apart on ungreased baking sheet.

Brush tops with egg yolk and water mixture.

Bake 10–12 minutes until golden brown. Serve warm.

Cool before storing.

*Exchange half and half cream for whipping cream.

Hint: Make scones in advance, cover and refrigerate up to 24 hours. Bake in preheated oven.

Freeze well.

Yield: 18

YOGURT SCONES

When I got married in 1979, I decided scones would be a regular bread item in our home. Easy to make, fun to eat.

2 cups	unbleached flour	500 mL
1 tsp	baking powder	5 mL
½ tsp	baking soda	2 mL
1 tsp	salt	5 mL
1 cup	plain yogurt	250 mL

Preheat oven to 425°F (220°C).

Mix all ingredients to make a soft dough. Pat to 1-inch (2.5 cm) thickness. Cut into 8 or 9 wedges and place on ungreased baking sheet.

Bake 15 minutes or until golden brown.

Serve hot.

BANNOCK

Bannock cooked on an open fire: a favourite at Brownie Camp, Fort McMurray, Alberta, 1967

1 cup	unbleached flour	250 mL
2 tsp	baking powder	10 mL
½ tsp	salt	2 mL
1 Tbsp	lard or butter, softened	15 mL
½ cup	water	125 mL
½ cup	raisins	125 mL

Mix well and shape into a cake. Place in greased cast iron frying pan over coals of a fire. Flip when the bottom turns brown. Brown on second side and serve.

*Food tastes great when cooked over a fire and
not dependent on skill or talent.*

GINGER TEA SCONES

2 cups	unbleached flour	500 mL
2 Tbsp	granulated sugar	30 mL
1 Tbsp	baking powder	15 mL
½ tsp	salt	2 mL
½–1 cup	candied ginger, chopped	125–250 mL
½ cup	cold butter, cubed	125 mL
1	egg	1
2/3 cup	milk or light cream	150 mL
	coarse sugar	

Preheat oven to 425°F (220°C).

Combine flour, sugar, baking powder and salt in Bosch Universal Kitchen Machine® bowl fitted with cookie paddles or wire whips and splash ring.

Cut butter into dry ingredients by pulsing the momentary switch until mixture resembles coarse crumbs. Add candied ginger and pulse gently to coat ginger with flour.

Lightly beat egg in small bowl, reserving 1 tablespoon (15 mL). Add milk to remaining beaten egg.

Add liquid ingredients to dry ingredients. Mix to obtain a slightly sticky dough.

Pour onto a lightly floured surface and gather dough into a ball. Knead gently a few times until dough is smooth. Roll dough to ½-inch (1.27 cm) thickness. Cut 2-inch (5 cm) circles with biscuit cutter and place 1-inch (2.5 cm) apart on ungreased baking sheet.

Brush tops with reserved egg. Sprinkle with coarse sugar.

Bake 12–14 minutes until golden brown. Serve warm.

Option: Form dough into two round discs and score into wedges with a pizza cutter or bench scraper.

Hint: Freeze shaped scones. Do not thaw. Bake in preheated 425°F (220°C) oven 15–18 minutes until golden brown.

Yield: 12–15

Ginger Tea Scones

CRANBERRY WALNUT SCONES

2 cups	unbleached flour	500 mL
¼ cup	brown sugar	60 mL
2 tsp	baking powder	10 mL
½ tsp	salt	2 mL
2 Tbsp	cold unsalted butter, cubed	30 mL
½ cup	fresh or dried cranberries, chopped	125 mL
¼ cup	walnuts, chopped	60 mL
1 cup	buttermilk	250 mL
1 Tbsp	skim milk	15 mL
1 Tbsp	brown sugar	15 mL

Preheat oven to 425°F (220°C).

In large bowl, stir flour, brown sugar, baking powder and salt together. With a pastry blender, cut butter into dry ingredients until the size of small peas. Stir in cranberries and walnuts.

Make a well in the centre and gradually stir in buttermilk with a fork, to form a ball. Knead gently. Do not overwork dough or it will be sticky and tough. Divide dough in two.

On a lightly floured surface, pat each portion into an 8-inch (20 cm) round, about ½- inch (1.27 cm) thick. Score each round into 8 triangles with a bench scraper or pizza wheel.

Place on ungreased baking sheet 1-inch (2.5 cm) apart.

Brush scones with milk and sprinkle with 1 Tbsp (15 mL) brown sugar.

Bake 14–18 minutes until golden brown. Serve warm.

Cool before storing.

Yield: 16

Cranberry Walnut Scones

POPPY SEED LOAF

2 ½ cups	sifted, fresh ground whole wheat flour*	625 mL
½ cup	unbleached flour	125 mL
2 cups	granulated sugar	500 mL
1 Tbsp	baking powder	15 mL
1 ½ tsp	salt	7 mL
3	eggs	3
1 ½ cups	milk	375 mL
1 cup	canola or vegetable oil	250 mL
2 Tbsp	poppy seeds	30 mL
1 Tbsp	grated lemon peel (zest)	15 mL
1 ½ tsp	almond extract	7 mL
1 ½ tsp	pure vanilla	7 mL
½ tsp	lemon extract	2 mL

GLAZE (Optional):

¾ cup	confectioner's (icing) sugar	175 mL
¼ cup	orange juice	60 mL
½ tsp	almond extract	2 mL
½ tsp	pure vanilla	2 mL

Preheat oven to 350°F (180°C).

In large bowl, combine flours, sugar, baking powder and salt. In a separate mixing bowl, whisk eggs, milk, oil, poppy seeds, lemon zest and flavourings. Stir wet mixture into dry ingredients. Transfer batter into greased 9 x 5 x 3-inch (23 x 13 x 8 cm) loaf pans.

Bake 55–60 minutes or until cake tester, inserted in middle of loaf, comes out clean.

Cool 10 minutes before removing from pans. Combine glaze ingredients, drizzle over loaves and cool on wire rack.

*Sift bran and germ from fresh ground whole wheat flour using a very fine sieve.

Bosch Universal Kitchen Machine® Method: Fit bowl with wire whips or cookie paddles and splash ring. Mix wet ingredients. Add dry ingredients. Position lids on mixing bowl. Pulse to incorporate dry ingredients. Pour batter into greased loaf pans and proceed.

Yield: 2

CRANBERRY NUT BREAD

Cranberries, nuts and chocolate are fabulous in quick breads. I created this recipe in 1980 to enjoy this combination.

1	egg	1
⅓ cup	butter, melted	75 mL
1 cup	milk	250 mL
2 tsp	vinegar	10 mL
2 cups	whole wheat flour (fresh ground)	500 mL
½ cup	granulated sugar	125 mL
1 ½ tsp	baking powder	7 mL
½ tsp	salt	2 mL
½ tsp	baking soda	2 mL
1 tsp	grated orange rind	5 mL
1 cup	cranberries, chopped	250 mL
½ cup	walnuts, chopped	125 mL
1 cup	semi-sweet chocolate chips or chunks	250 mL

Preheat oven to 350°F (180°C).

In medium-sized mixing bowl, beat egg, butter, milk and vinegar. Add remaining ingredients and mix until dry ingredients are moistened. Spoon into greased and floured 9 x 5 x 3-inch (23 x 13 x 8 cm) loaf pan.

Bake 55–60 minutes or until cake tester, inserted in middle of loaf, comes out clean.

Remove from pan. Sprinkle with icing sugar or doughnut sugar (available in specialty food stores).

Cool on wire rack before storing.

Bosch Universal Kitchen Machine® Method: Fit bowl with wire whips or cookie paddles and splash ring. Mix wet ingredients. Add dry ingredients. Position lids on mixing bowl. Pulse to incorporate dry ingredients. Pour batter into greased loaf pans and proceed.

Yield: 1

Bosch Universal Plus
Kitchen Machine®

NutriMill Flour Mill®

Bosch Universal Plus Kitchen Machine®
(with mixing accessories)

46

Cakes

BARB'S CARROT CAKE

I developed this recipe in 1975. Don't wait for a special occasion to bake this delicious, moist cake.

1 ½ cups	canola or vegetable oil*	375 mL
3	eggs	3
1 ½ cups	granulated sugar	375 mL
2 cups	whole wheat flour	500 mL
2 tsp	baking soda	10 mL
½ tsp	salt	2 mL
2 ½ tsp	cinnamon	12 mL
Dash	nutmeg	dash
2 cups	grated carrots	500 mL
1 cup	walnuts, chopped	250 mL
1 cup	drained, crushed pineapple* or 1, 14-oz (398 mL) can, drained	250 mL

Preheat oven to 350°F (180°C).

In Bosch Universal Kitchen Machine® bowl equipped with wire whips or cookie paddles, beat oil, eggs and sugar. Add remaining ingredients and pulse momentary switch until mixed.

Pour into greased and floured 10-inch (25 cm) tube pan, Bundt pan or 10-inch (25 cm) springform pan.

Bake 60 minutes or until cake tester comes out clean.

Cool 5–10 minutes in pan. Invert pan onto cooling rack to remove cake and cool completely. Drizzle liberally with *Icing Sugar Glaze*.

*Replace ¾ cup (175 mL) oil with ¾ cup (175 mL) unsweetened applesauce.

*Reserve pineapple juice for icing or as part of oil measurement.

Option: Bake in 13 x 9 x 2-inch (33 x 23 x 5 cm) pan 45–55 minutes. Cool and frost with *Cream Cheese Icing*.

CREAM CHEESE ICING

2, 8-oz	packages cream cheese	454 g
1 cup	confectioner's (icing) sugar	250 mL
1 tsp	vanilla	5 mL

Combine ingredients and beat well. Add pineapple juice, if desired, and beat well. Ice cooled cake. Sprinkle with ¾ cup (175 mL) shredded coconut.

Wire racks are important for air flow while cooling baked goods.

Barb's Carrot Cake

APPLE CAKE

Adapted from my friend Gertie's recipe, 1980.

2 cups	granulated sugar	500 mL
4	eggs	4
1 cup	canola or vegetable oil	250 mL
1 tsp	vanilla	5 mL
3 cups	whole wheat flour or unbleached flour	750 mL
1 tsp	baking soda	5 mL
1 tsp	salt	5 mL
1 tsp	cinnamon	5 mL
2 cups	diced apples	500 mL
1 cup	dark raisins	250 mL
1 ¼ cups	chopped walnuts	310 mL

Preheat oven to 350°F (180°C).

In Bosch Universal Kitchen Machine® bowl equipped with batter whips or cookie paddles, beat sugar, eggs, oil and vanilla. Add flour, baking soda, salt and cinnamon. Mix.

Add apples, raisins and walnuts and mix to blend. Pour batter into greased 10-inch (25 cm) Bundt pan.

Sprinkle with ¼ cup (60 mL) chopped walnuts before baking, if desired.

Bake 70 minutes or until cake tester comes out clean.

Cool 5–10 minutes before removing from pan. Cool on wire rack. Spoon glaze on cake and let drizzle down the sides.

GLAZE

1 ⅓ cups	confectioner's (icing) sugar	325 mL
2 Tbsp	apple juice or water	30 mL

Mix icing sugar and apple juice until smooth. Spoon over cake.

I leave skins on the apples for extra fibre,
colour and nutrition in this easy cake.

APPLE COFFEE CAKE

Adapted from my friend Gertie's recipe, 1979.

½ cup	butter, softened	125 mL
1 cup	granulated sugar	250 mL
2	eggs	2
1 tsp	vanilla	5 mL
1 tsp	maple extract	5 mL
1 cup	sour cream	250 mL
2 cups	unbleached flour	500 mL
1 tsp	baking soda	5 mL
1 tsp	baking powder	5 mL
½ tsp	salt	2 mL
2	medium tart apples, peeled, cored, chopped	2

TOPPING

½ cup	packed brown sugar	125 mL
2 Tbsp	butter	30 mL
1 tsp	cinnamon	5 mL
½ tsp	nutmeg	2 mL
½ cup	walnuts, chopped	125 mL

Preheat oven to 375°F (190°C).

Grease and flour 10-inch (25 cm) coffee cake (tube) pan and set aside.

In Bosch Universal Kitchen Machine® bowl equipped with wire whips, cream butter, sugar, eggs and flavourings. Add remaining ingredients and mix.

Combine topping ingredients in small bowl.

Pour half the batter into greased pan and sprinkle with half the topping crumbs.

Spread remaining batter in pan and sprinkle with remaining crumbs.

Bake 40 minutes or until cake tester comes out clean.

Cool in pan 10 minutes before turning cake onto wire rack or serving platter to cool completely.

BANANA NUT CAKE

Adapted from my sister-in-law Cheryl's recipe, 1979.

½ cup	butter	125 mL
1 cup	granulated sugar	250 mL
2	eggs	2
1 tsp	vanilla	5 mL
1 cup	mashed bananas*	250 mL
¼ tsp	salt	1 mL
2 tsp	baking powder	10 mL
1 tsp	baking soda	5 mL
¼ cup	boiling water	60 mL
2 cups	whole wheat, spelt or barley flour	500 mL
1 cup	chopped nuts or chocolate chips	250 mL

Preheat oven to 350°F (180°C).

In Bosch Universal Kitchen Machine® bowl equipped with wire whips, cream butter, sugar, eggs and vanilla. Add bananas, salt and baking powder. Mix well.

Dissolve baking soda in boiling water and add alternately with the flour.

Add nuts or chocolate chips and gently pulse momentary switch to disperse ingredients evenly.

Spread in greased 9 x 9-inch (23 x 23 cm) cake pan.

Bake 35–40 minutes until cake tester comes out clean.

Cool on wire rack.

Prep time: less than 5 minutes!

CRANBERRY CAKE

Adapted from my friend Carmen's recipe, 1980.

1	egg	1
½ cup	blackstrap molasses	125 mL
½ cup	granulated sugar	125 mL
½ cup	hot water	125 mL
½ tsp	salt	2 mL
1 ½ Tbsp	baking soda	22 mL
1 ½ cups	unbleached flour	375 mL
1 ½ cups	whole raw cranberries	375 mL

Preheat oven to 350°F (180°C).

Beat egg, molasses, sugar, hot water, salt and baking soda in Bosch Universal Kitchen Machine® bowl equipped with wire whips. Add flour and cranberries. Blend by pulsing momentary switch.

Bake 35 minutes in greased 13 x 9 x 2-inch (33 x 23 x 5 cm) pan.

Serve warm or cold with hot *Butter Sauce*.

BUTTER SAUCE

½ cup	butter	125 mL
1 cup	granulated sugar	250 mL
½ cup	cream or sweetened condensed milk	125 mL
	Almond or vanilla extract	

Bring butter, sugar and cream to a boil. Do not scorch. Add flavouring and stir.

Option: Add small amount of cranberry sauce before boiling.

CHOCOLATE LOVERS' CAKE

Adapted from Natural Nine Cookbook (out-of-print), 1984.

3 cups	whole wheat flour	750 mL
1 ¾ cups	granulated sugar	425 mL
½ cup	Dutch cocoa	125 mL
1 Tbsp	baking soda	15 mL
1 tsp	baking powder	5 mL
1 tsp	salt	5 mL
2	eggs	2
2 cups	buttermilk	500 mL
½ cup	canola or vegetable oil	125 mL
½ cup	applesauce	125 mL
1 Tbsp	vanilla	15 mL
1 cup	hot water	250 mL

Preheat oven to 350°F (180°C).

Combine all dry ingredients in Bosch Universal Kitchen Machine® bowl equipped with wire whips and lids. Add wet ingredients, except water, and mix. Add water and mix well. Pour into greased and lightly floured 13 x 9 x 2-inch (33 x 23 x 5 cm) cake pan or three greased 9-inch (23 cm) pans.

Bake 13 x 9 x 2-inch (33 x 23 x 5 cm) cake 45–50 minutes or round cakes 30–35 minutes until cake tester comes out clean. Cool, ice and decorate, as desired.

Option: Bake 24 cupcakes in grease-proof paper or foil cups 25–30 minutes until cake tester comes out clean when inserted into the middle of a cupcake.

Note: Substitute canola or vegetable oil if applesauce is not available.

Chocolate Lovers' Cake batter is very fluid (liquid); however, bran and germ in whole wheat flour absorbs moisture during baking. The bowl scraper accessory scrapes the bowl while mixing.

Prep time: less than 5 minutes!

Line round cake pans with parchment paper to remove cakes with ease, when inverted.

BLACK FOREST CAKE

Bake *Chocolate Lovers'* Cake in round pans.

CHERRY SAUCE FOR BLACK FOREST CAKE

8 cups	cherries	2000 mL
½ cup	water	125 mL
¾ cup	granulated sugar	175 mL
½ tsp	almond extract	2 mL
	cornstarch	

Combine first 3 ingredients in large saucepan. Simmer on medium-low heat 15–20 minutes, stirring occasionally. Add extract and thicken with cornstarch.

ASSEMBLE BLACK FOREST CAKE

Invert one cake layer onto serving platter. Spread with whipped cream and half the *Cherry Sauce*. Repeat with second layer.

Top third layer with whipped cream.

Garnish layered cake with shaved chocolate and whole cherries.

Variation: Soak whole cherries in kirsch before simmering.

Chocolate and cherries: Two of my favourite foods.
Bake this! Call me!

PRIZED COFFEE CAKE

Adapted from my friend Gertie's recipe, 1980.

⅔ cup	granulated sugar	150 mL
2 Tbsp	shortening	30 mL
1	egg	1
⅔ cup	milk	150 mL
1 tsp	vanilla	5 mL
1 ¼ cups	unbleached flour	310 mL
2 tsp	baking powder	10 mL
½ tsp	salt	2 mL
1 tsp	cinnamon	5 mL
1 cup	nuts, chopped	250 mL
¼ cup	brown sugar	60 mL
¼ cup	granulated sugar	60 mL

Preheat oven to 350°F (180°C).

In Bosch Universal Kitchen Machine® bowl equipped with wire whips or cookie paddles, mix sugar, shortening, egg, milk and vanilla.

Add flour, baking powder, salt, and pulse momentary switch until ingredients are incorporated.

Pour half the mixture into greased 8-inch (20 cm) pan.

In small bowl, mix cinnamon, nuts and sugars and sprinkle on batter. Top with remaining batter.

Bake 25–30 minutes until cake tester comes out clean.

Cool on wire rack.

CITRUS BUNDT CAKE

¾ cup	butter	175 mL
1 ¼ cups	granulated sugar	310 mL
3	eggs	3
2 tsp	grated orange rind (zest)	10 mL
2 cups	unbleached or barley flour	500 mL
1 cup	oat bran	250 mL
4 tsp	baking powder	20 mL
½ tsp	salt	2 mL
1 ¼ cups	milk	310 mL

GLAZE

½ cup	granulated sugar	125 mL
2 Tbsp	orange juice	30 mL
1 Tbsp	lemon juice	15 mL

Preheat oven to 350°F (180°C). Grease and flour 10-inch (25 cm) Bundt pan.

In Bosch Universal Kitchen Machine® bowl equipped with wire whips, cream butter, sugar and eggs. Add dry ingredients alternately with milk, mixing briefly after each addition. Pour batter into prepared pan.

Bake 45–50 minutes until cake tester comes out clean.

Combine glaze ingredients in small bowl.

Cool 5 minutes before inverting onto cooling rack. Pour glaze over warm cake.

Cool completely.

Zest citrus fruits with a very fine grater. Dry on parchment paper.
Use half the amount required when replacing fresh zest with dried zest (peel).

GINGER SPICE CAKE

2 ¼ cups	unbleached flour	560 mL
1 cup	brown sugar	250 mL
¾ cup	candied ginger, chopped	175 mL
¼ cup	maple syrup	60 mL
¼ tsp	allspice	1 mL
¼ tsp	ginger	1 mL
1 tsp	cinnamon	5 mL
½ tsp	nutmeg	2 mL
1 tsp	baking soda	5 mL
¾ cup	buttermilk	175 mL
1	egg	1

Preheat oven to 350°F (180°C).

Mix dry ingredients. Add egg and buttermilk and mix well.

Pour into well-greased, floured 9 x 5 x 3-inch (23 x 13 x 8 cm) loaf pan.

Bake 45–55 minutes until cake tester comes out clean.

Cool on wire rack.

OATMEAL RYE CAKE

Adapted from Natural Nine Cookbook (out-of-print), 1984.

½ cup	butter, softened	125 mL
1 cup	brown sugar	250 mL
2	eggs	2
1 tsp	vanilla	5 mL
3 Tbsp	barley flour	45 mL
1 ¼ cups	rye flour	310 mL
1 cup	large flake rolled oats	250 mL
1 tsp	baking soda	5 mL
½ tsp	salt	2 mL
¾ tsp	cinnamon	3 mL
¼ tsp	nutmeg	1 mL
1 ¼ cups	water	310 mL

Preheat oven to 350°F (180°C).

In Bosch Universal Kitchen Machine® bowl equipped with wire whips and splash ring, cream butter, sugar, eggs and vanilla. Combine dry ingredients.

Alternately add dry ingredients and water to the creamed mixture (batter will be thin).

Pour into greased 13 x 9 x 2-inch (33 x 23 x 5 cm) pan.

Bake 30 minutes. Spread *Brown Sugar Frosting* on hot cake. Broil 4–5 minutes until golden brown.

BROWN SUGAR FROSTING

½ cup	brown sugar	125 mL
⅓ cup	butter, softened	75 mL
4 ½ Tbsp	light cream	67 mL
1 cup	coconut, medium unsweetened	250 mL

Mix ingredients until well blended.

Spread on hot cake with offset spatula.

PLUM CAKE

Adapted from my friend Gertie's recipe, 1979.

2	eggs	2
1 cup	granulated sugar	250 mL
¾ cup	milk	175 mL
1 tsp	vanilla	5 mL
2 cups	unbleached flour*	500 mL
½ tsp	salt	2 mL
2 tsp	baking powder	10 mL
2 cups	plums, diced	500 mL

TOPPING

1 cup	granulated sugar	250 mL
½ cup	unbleached flour	125 mL
1 tsp	cinnamon	5 mL
½ cup	butter	125 mL

Preheat oven to 350°F (180°C).

In Bosch Universal Kitchen Machine® bowl equipped with wire whips and splash ring, mix eggs, sugar, milk and vanilla. Add dry ingredients and mix.

Spread in greased pie or 9 x 9-inch (23 x 23 cm) square pan. Cover with washed, pitted and diced plums.

Topping: Use pastry blender or fork to cut butter into sugar, flour and cinnamon until mixture resembles coarse crumbs. Sprinkle topping over plums.

Bake 45 minutes. Serve with ice cream or whipped cream.

*Exchange fresh ground whole wheat flour, spelt, Kamut® or barley flour for unbleached flour.

Prep time: less than 5 minutes!

POPPY SEED BUNDT

1 cup	butter, room temperature	250 mL
1 ½ cups	granulated sugar	375 mL
5	eggs, separated	5
2 ½ cups	hard white wheat flour (sift off bran and germ)	625 mL
1 tsp	baking soda	5 mL
1 tsp	baking powder	5 mL
1 cup	buttermilk	250 mL
¾ cup	poppy seeds	175 mL
1 tsp	almond extract	5 mL
½ cup	granulated sugar	125 mL
1 tsp	cinnamon	5 mL

Preheat oven to 350°F (180°C). Grease and flour large Bundt pan.

Cream butter and sugar in Bosch Universal Kitchen Machine® bowl equipped with wire whips.

Add egg yolks and cream until batter is pale yellow.

Sift flour, baking soda and baking powder into small bowl. Pour poppy seeds and extract into buttermilk.

Add half of flour mixture and buttermilk mixture to butter batter. Mix. Add remaining flour mixture and buttermilk mixture to butter batter. Mix.

In a separate bowl, beat egg whites until stiff and fold evenly into batter by pulsing momentary switch.

Pour half the batter into prepared pan. Combine ½ cup (125 mL) sugar and 1 tsp (5 mL) cinnamon and sprinkle on batter. Pour remaining batter into pan and spread evenly.

Bake 60 minutes or until cake tester comes out clean.

Cool 10 minutes in pan before inverting onto serving platter.

FROSTED PUMPKIN SLAB

Adapted from my friend Anne's recipe, 1982.

4	eggs	4
1 cup	canola or vegetable oil	250 mL
2 cups	granulated sugar	500 mL
1 cup	pumpkin puree	250 mL
2 cups	unbleached flour	500 mL
1 tsp	baking powder	5 mL
1 tsp	baking soda	5 mL
2 tsp	cinnamon	10 mL
½ tsp	salt	2 mL
1 cup	chopped nuts or raisins	250 mL

Preheat oven to 350°F (180°C).

Mix first 4 ingredients in Bosch Universal Kitchen Machine® bowl equipped with wire whips, bowl scraper and splash ring.

Add dry ingredients, except nuts or raisins, and mix to incorporate.

Add chopped nuts or raisins and pulse momentary switch to mix.

Pour into greased 10 ½ x 15 ½ x 1-inch (27 x 39 x 2.5 cm) baking sheet (jellyroll pan).

Bake 20–25 minutes until lightly brown and cake tester comes out clean.

While warm, spread with frosting, or serve with confectioner's (icing) sugar or whipped cream, when cool.

Prep time: less than 5 minutes!

FROSTING

3 oz	cream cheese, softened	85 g
6 Tbsp	butter, softened	90 mL
¾ lb	confectioner's (icing) sugar	340 g
1 tsp	vanilla	5 mL
1 tsp	milk	5 mL

Beat ingredients until smooth and spread on warm cake. Add extra milk, if necessary.

Sprinkle frosting with cinnamon, if desired.

GLAZED PUMPKIN CAKE

1 cup	unsalted butter, softened	250 mL
½ cup	granulated sugar	125 mL
1 ½ cups	lightly packed brown sugar	375 mL
4	eggs	4
2 tsp	vanilla	10 mL
2 cups	pumpkin puree	500 mL
3 cups	unbleached or white wheat flour	750 mL
1 ½ tsp	baking powder	7 mL
½ tsp	baking soda	2 mL
¾ tsp	salt	3 mL
1 Tbsp	cinnamon	15 mL
1 tsp	nutmeg	5 mL
1 tsp	ginger	5 mL
½ tsp	allspice	2 mL
½ cup	pecans, coarsely chopped	125 mL

GLAZE

¼ cup	packed brown sugar	60 mL
¼ cup	maple syrup	60 mL
2 tsp	vanilla	10 mL
1 Tbsp	unsalted butter	15 mL

Preheat oven to 350°F (180°C). Lightly grease and flour large Bundt pan. Sift dry ingredients and set aside.

In Bosch Universal Kitchen Machine® bowl equipped with wire whips and bowl scraper, cream butter until light and fluffy. Add sugars, eggs and vanilla and beat well. On speed #1, alternately beat in ⅓ flour mixture, ½ pumpkin puree, ⅓ flour mixture, remaining pumpkin puree and remaining flour mixture.

Add nuts and mix with momentary switch. Pour batter into prepared pan and smooth gently.

Bake 70 minutes or until cake tester comes out clean. The cake will appear to have pulled away from the edge of the pan.

Cool in pan on wire rack, 5–10 minutes before carefully inverting onto rack or serving platter.

Glaze: Cook sugar, syrup and vanilla in small saucepan, on medium heat. Bring to boil, stirring constantly, cook 1 minute. Remove from heat, add butter and stir to melt. Using pastry brush, paint glaze over warm cake until glaze has been absorbed.

Cool completely. Wrap well to store.

RHUBARB SOUR MILK CAKE

Adapted from Rena's recipe, 1978. I lived in her home one summer during university and have wonderful memories of the recipes she shared

½ cup	butter	125 mL
¾–1 cup	brown sugar	175–250 mL
2	eggs	2
1 tsp	vanilla	5 mL
2 cups	fresh ground whole wheat flour	500 mL
1 cup	sour milk*	250 mL
1 tsp	baking soda	5 mL
1 tsp	salt	5 mL
1 ½ cups	rhubarb, finely chopped, fresh or frozen	375 mL

TOPPING

½ cup	brown sugar	125 mL
1 tsp	cinnamon	5 mL

Preheat oven to 350°F (180°C).

In Bosch Universal Kitchen Machine® bowl equipped with wire whips and splash ring, cream butter, sugar, eggs and vanilla.

Add flour, sour milk, baking soda and salt. Mix well.

Add rhubarb and pulse momentary switch to mix.

Pour into greased 13 x 9 x 2-inch (33 x 23 x 5 cm) pan.

Mix topping ingredients and sprinkle on batter.

Bake 45 minutes.

Serve with ice cream or whipped cream.

*To sour fresh milk, pour 1 Tbsp (15 mL) vinegar or lemon juice into measuring cup before adding milk.

Prep time: less than 5 minutes!

A favourite all year!

Rhubarb Sour Milk Cake

RHUBARB COFFEE CAKE

Adapted from my friend Gertie's recipe, 1980.

2 cups	diced rhubarb	500 mL
¼ cup	granulated sugar	60 mL
½ cup	butter, softened	125 mL
⅔ cup	granulated sugar	150 mL
2	eggs	2
1 ½ tsp	pure vanilla	7 mL
½ cup	spelt flour	125 mL
1 cup	unbleached flour	250 mL
1 tsp	baking powder	5 mL
⅛ tsp	baking soda	0.5 mL
½ tsp	salt	2 mL
¾ cup	buttermilk	175 mL
2 Tbsp	brown sugar	30 mL
½ tsp	cinnamon	2 mL

Preheat oven to 350°F (180°C).

Combine rhubarb and ¼ cup (60 mL) sugar in small bowl. Set aside.

In Bosch Universal Kitchen Machine® bowl equipped with cookie paddles, cream butter and ⅔ cup (150 mL) sugar until light and fluffy. Add eggs and vanilla and beat well.

Combine flour, baking powder, baking soda and salt and add to creamed mixture alternately with buttermilk. Fold in rhubarb.

Pour into greased 9-inch (23 cm) square baking pan.

Combine brown sugar and cinnamon and sprinkle over batter.

Bake 25–30 minutes until cake tester comes out clean.

Yield: 9–12 servings

Chop and freeze rhubarb for treats any time of the year.

SPICY TOMATO SOUP CAKE

Adapted from my mom's recipe, 1970.

1 ⅔ cups	sifted whole wheat flour	400 mL
⅓ cup	barley flour	75 mL
1 ¼ cups	granulated sugar	310 mL
4 tsp	baking powder	20 mL
1 tsp	baking soda	5 mL
1 ½ tsp	allspice	7 mL
1 tsp	cinnamon	5 mL
½ tsp	cloves	2 mL
1, 10-oz can	condensed tomato soup	284 mL
½ cup	soft butter	125 mL
2	eggs	2
¼ cup	water	60 mL

Preheat oven to 350°F (180°C).

In large mixing bowl or Bosch Universal Kitchen Machine® bowl equipped with wire whips or batter whips and lids, combine dry ingredients. Add tomato soup, butter, eggs and water and mix well. Pour batter into greased and floured 13 x 9 x 2-inch (33 x 23 x 5 cm) cake pan.

Bake 35 minutes or until cake springs back when lightly touched.

Cool and frost with *Cream Cheese Frosting*.

CREAM CHEESE FROSTING

4 oz	cream cheese, softened	125 g
¼ cup	butter, softened	60 mL
1 tsp	vanilla	5 mL
2–2 ½ cups	confectioner's (icing) sugar	500–625 mL

Beat cream cheese, butter and vanilla until smooth.

Add icing sugar and beat to obtain desired consistency.

Spread evenly over cooled *Spicy Tomato Soup Cake*.

A childhood favourite!

WACKY CHOCOLATE CAKE

Adapted from Anne's recipe, a university roommate, 1976.

1 ½ cups	unbleached flour	375 mL
1 tsp	baking powder	5 mL
½ tsp	salt	2 mL
1 cup	granulated sugar	250 mL
1 tsp	baking soda	5 mL
4 Tbsp	Dutch cocoa	60 mL

Preheat oven to 350°F (180°C). Grease and flour 9-inch (23 cm) round cake pan.

Combine ingredients in medium-sized mixing bowl. Make three holes in mixture.

Put 1 tsp (5 mL) vanilla in one hole, 5 Tbsp (75 mL) softened butter in second hole and 1 Tbsp (15 mL) vinegar in third hole.

Pour 1 cup (250 mL) warm water over mixture. Stir to combine. Pour into prepared pan.

Bake 20–25 minutes until cake tester comes out clean.

Cool on wire rack and frost with *Chocolate Icing*.

Prep time: less than 5 minutes!

CHOCOLATE ICING

1 cup	confectioner's (icing) sugar	250 mL
1 Tbsp	butter	15 mL
1 Tbsp	Dutch cocoa	15 mL
1 Tbsp	hot water	15 mL
1 tsp	vanilla	5 mL

Combine all ingredients in small bowl. Beat until smooth. Spread on cooled cake.

WHITE ICING

Follow recipe for *Chocolate Icing*, omitting cocoa.

A favourite recipe from a university roommate!
Easy to assemble. Moist and delicious!

Cookies & Squares

GERRY'S FAVOURITE COOKIES (1986)

1 cup	butter, softened	250 mL
½ cup	brown sugar	125 mL
½ cup	granulated sugar	125 mL
1 tsp	vanilla	5 mL
2	eggs	2
1 cup	whole wheat flour (less 2 Tbsp)	220 mL
1 cup	triticale flour	250 mL
1 tsp	baking powder	5 mL
1 tsp	baking soda	5 mL
1 cup	coconut	250 mL
1 cup	rolled oats	250 mL
1 cup	raisins or cranberries	250 mL
1 cup	chocolate or yogurt chips	250 mL
¾ cup	sunflower seeds	175 mL
½ cup	sesame seeds	125 mL
⅓ cup	flax seeds	75 mL
⅓ cup	whole millet	75 mL

Preheat oven to 350°F (180°C).

In Bosch Universal Kitchen Machine® bowl equipped with cookie paddles and splash ring, beat butter, sugars, vanilla and eggs.

Add remaining ingredients and mix well.

Roll into balls or shape with 35mm spring-loaded scoop. Place on greased baking sheets and flatten slightly with a fork dipped in water.

Bake 10 minutes.

Yield: 84 - 35mm
      68 - 40mm

Many years ago, this recipe changed from Barb's Favourite Cookies to Gerry's (staff member for over 30 years) Favourite Cookies after she repeatedly mentioned they were her favourite, too! Delicious and nutritious!

Gerry's Favourite Cookies

OATMEAL NUT COOKIES

I created this recipe after organizing my baking cupboard, 1981.

¾ cup	butter, softened	175 mL
½ cup	brown sugar	125 mL
¼ cup	granulated sugar	60 mL
1	egg	1
1 tsp	vanilla	5 mL
¾ cup	whole wheat flour	175 mL
¾ cup	oat flour	175 mL
½ tsp	baking powder	2 mL
1 cup	rolled oats	250 mL
1 cup	barley flakes	250 mL
1 cup	flaked coconut	250 mL
1 cup	raisins	250 mL
¾ cup	pecans, chopped (optional)	175 mL

Preheat oven to 375°F (190°C).

In Bosch Universal Kitchen Machine® bowl equipped with batter whips or cookie paddles and splash ring, beat butter, sugars, egg and vanilla.

Add remaining ingredients and mix to combine.

Use 39mm spring-loaded scoop to drop dough onto lightly greased or parchment-lined baking sheets.

Bake 10–12 minutes until lightly browned.

Cool on wire rack.

GINGER RYE COOKIES

I created this recipe to use various rolled grains, 1979.

1 cup	butter, softened	250 mL
¾ cup	granulated sugar	175 mL
1 Tbsp	corn syrup	15 mL
½ tsp	baking soda	2 mL
2 Tbsp	hot water	30 mL
1 cup	rye flour	250 mL
2 ¼ cups	rye flakes	560 mL
2 heaping tsp	ginger	10 mL

Preheat oven to 350°F (180°C).

Cream butter, sugar and syrup. Add remaining ingredients and mix well.

Roll into small balls or shape with 35mm spring-loaded scoop and place on greased baking sheets. Flatten balls with a fork.

Bake 13–18 minutes.

Cool on wire racks.

VARIATIONS:

Rye flour and flakes may be replaced with barley, oats, spelt, triticale or whole wheat flour and flakes.

Prep time: less than 5 minutes!

SOFT GINGER COOKIES

¾ cup	butter or shortening, softened	175 mL
1 cup	granulated sugar	250 mL
2 tsp	ginger	10 mL
1 tsp	baking soda	5 mL
¾ tsp	cinnamon	3 mL
½ tsp	cloves	2 mL
1	egg	1
¼ cup	blackstrap molasses	60 mL
2 ¼ cups	triticale or unbleached flour	560 mL
½ cup	raisins	125 mL
¼ cup	coarse or granulated sugar	60 mL

Preheat oven to 350°F (180°C).

In Bosch Universal Kitchen Machine® bowl equipped with cookie paddles and splash ring, beat butter 30 seconds.

Add 1 cup (250 mL) sugar, ginger, baking soda, cinnamon and cloves. Beat. Beat in egg and molasses.

Add flour and raisins and mix to combine.

Use 39mm spring-loaded scoop to shape balls, roll in ¼ cup (60 mL) coarse or granulated sugar and place 2 ½ inches (6.5 cm) apart on parchment-lined baking sheets.

Bake 10 minutes or until light brown. Do not overbake.

Let rest on baking sheets 2 minutes.

Transfer to wire racks and cool completely.

Yield: 24

THREE GINGER COOKIES

¾ cup	butter, softened	175 mL
1 cup	packed brown sugar	250 mL
¼ cup	blackstrap molasses	60 mL
1	egg	1
4 tsp	candied ginger, finely chopped	20 mL
2 ¼ cups	unbleached flour	560 mL
2 tsp	ground ginger	10 mL
1 tsp	baking soda	5 mL
½ tsp	salt	2 mL
½ cup	crystallised ginger, finely chopped	125 mL

Preheat oven to 350°F (180°C).

In Bosch Universal Kitchen Machine® bowl equipped with cookie paddles and splash ring, beat butter, sugar, molasses and egg. Add remaining ingredients and mix well.

Drop mounds of dough over entire surface of greased 15 ½ x 10 ½ x 1-inch (39 x 27 x 2.5 cm) jelly roll pan. Press dough evenly and smooth surface with a metal spatula.

Bake 13–15 minutes until lightly browned.

Cool in pan on wire rack for 15 minutes.

Cut into bars and transfer to wire rack to cool completely.

Option: Shape cookies with 35mm spring-loaded scoop with release and bake 10–12 minutes until light brown.

Yield: 60

BUTTERSCOTCH OAT COOKIES

Adapted from Natural Nine Cookbook (out-of-print), 1984.

1 ½ cups	butter, softened	375 mL
1 ¾ cups	brown sugar	425 mL
2 Tbsp	vinegar	30 mL
1, 13-oz can	evaporated milk	354 mL
4	eggs	4
8 cups	oat flour	2000 mL
2 tsp	baking powder	10 mL
2 tsp	baking soda	10 mL
2 cups	raisins	500 mL
2 cups	butterscotch chips	500 mL
1 cup	chocolate chips	250 mL
2 cups	shredded coconut	500 mL

Preheat oven to 350°F (180°C).

In Bosch Universal Kitchen Machine® bowl equipped with cookie paddles and splash ring, cream butter and sugar.

Pour vinegar into evaporated milk and add to creamed mixture. Add eggs and mix.

Add remaining ingredients and mix well.

Drop onto lightly greased baking sheets with 39mm spring-loaded scoop.

Bake 8–10 minutes.

Cool on wire racks.

Yield: 96

Use your time efficiently . . . bake more.

TRITICALE SESAME COOKIES

I've been making these since 1980. A great cookie with fresh ground flour.

3 Tbsp	canola or vegetable oil	45 mL
1 cup	brown sugar	250 mL
2	eggs	2
1 ½ tsp	vanilla	7 mL
1 ¾ cups	triticale flakes	425 mL
1 cup	triticale or whole wheat flour	250 mL
¼ cup	wheat germ	60 mL
1 tsp	baking soda	5 mL
¼ tsp	salt	1 mL
¼ cup	sesame seeds	60 mL
½ cup	walnuts, chopped	125 mL

Preheat oven to 350°F (180°C).

In Bosch Universal Kitchen Machine® bowl equipped with batter whips or cookie paddles and splash ring, mix oil, sugar, eggs and vanilla.

Add remaining ingredients and mix to combine.

Use 35mm spring-loaded scoop to drop batter onto parchment-lined or greased baking sheets.

Bake 9–11 minutes until golden brown.

Prep time: less than 5 minutes!

ALMOND SPICE COOKIES

½ cup	butter, softened	125 mL
½ cup	granulated sugar	125 mL
1	egg	1
½ tsp	almond extract	2 mL
1 ¼ cups	unbleached flour	310 mL
¼ tsp	cinnamon	1 mL
¼ tsp	nutmeg	1 mL
¼ tsp	cloves	1 mL
¼ tsp	baking powder	1 mL
Pinch	salt	pinch
½ cup	almonds, chopped	125 mL

Preheat oven to 350°F (180°C).

In Bosch Universal Kitchen Machine® bowl equipped with batter whips or cookie paddles, cream butter and sugar.

Add egg and extract and mix well.

Combine dry ingredients and add to creamed mixture. Mix well.

Use 39mm spring-loaded scoop to drop tablespoon (15 mL)-sized batter onto parchment-lined or greased baking sheets.

Bake 10–12 minutes until edges are golden brown.

Yield: 36, 2-inch (5 cm)

SUGAR AND SPICE COFFEE COOKIES

½ cup	butter, softened (no substitutes)	125 mL
¼ cup	shortening	60 mL
1 cup	granulated sugar	250 mL
½ cup	brown sugar	125 mL
1	egg	1
1 tsp	baking powder	5 mL
1 tsp	cinnamon	5 mL
¼ tsp	salt	1 mL
2 Tbsp	instant coffee powder	30 mL
1 Tbsp	hot water	15 mL
2 cups	unbleached flour	500 mL

Coffee Topping
Coffee beans (optional)

Preheat oven to 375°F (190°C).

In Bosch Universal Kitchen Machine® bowl equipped with cookie paddles and splash ring, beat butter and shortening. Add sugars, egg, baking powder, cinnamon and salt. Beat well.

In small bowl, stir coffee powder and hot water and blend into sugar mixture. Add flour and combine.

Divide dough into thirds and shape each portion into 7 x 2-inch (18 x 5 cm) roll. Wrap each roll in plastic wrap or parchment paper and chill 2 hours until firm.

Cut each roll into 3/8-inch (9.5 mm) slices and place on parchment-lined or greased baking sheets approximately 2 inches (5 cm) apart. Sprinkle with coffee topping and gently press a coffee bean onto each dough slice.

Bake 9–10 minutes until edges are light brown. Cool on baking sheets 1 minute.

Transfer to wire racks and cool completely.

COFFEE TOPPING

¼ cup	granulated sugar	60 mL
1 tsp	instant coffee powder	5 mL

Mix in a small bowl.

Yield: 36

JUMBO RAISIN COOKIES

Adapted from Rena's recipe, 1978. I lived in her home one summer during university and have wonderful memories of the recipes she shared.

1 cup	water	250 mL
2 cups	raisins	500 mL

Boil water and raisins 5 minutes. Cool. Do not drain.

1 cup	butter, softened	250 mL
1 ½ cups	granulated sugar	375 mL
3	eggs	3
1 tsp	vanilla	5 mL
4 cups	whole wheat flour	1000 mL
1 tsp	baking powder	5 mL
1 tsp	baking soda	5 mL
1 tsp	salt	5 mL
1 ½ tsp	cinnamon	7 mL
¼ tsp	nutmeg	1 mL
¼ tsp	allspice	1 mL

Preheat oven to 375°F (190°C).

In Bosch Universal Kitchen Machine® bowl equipped with cookie paddles and splash ring, beat butter, sugar, eggs and vanilla.

Add remaining ingredients and raisin mixture. Mix well.

Drop by tablespoonfuls (15 mL) onto baking sheets.

Bake 12–15 minutes.

Cool on wire racks.

Yield: lots!

BARLEY PEANUT BUTTER COOKIES

Adapted from an old recipe in my recipe boxes, 1976.

½ cup	granulated sugar	125 mL
½ cup	brown sugar	125 mL
½ cup	butter, softened	125 mL
1	egg	1
⅔ cup	peanut butter	150 mL
1 ½ cups	barley flour*	375 mL
¼ cup	flaxseeds, cracked	60 mL
½ tsp	baking powder	2 mL
½ tsp	baking soda	2 mL
¼ tsp	salt	1 mL

Preheat oven to 350°F (180°C).

In Bosch Universal Kitchen Machine® bowl equipped with cookie paddles and splash ring, cream sugars, butter, egg and peanut butter.

Add remaining ingredients and mix to incorporate.

Roll batter into 1-inch (2.5 cm) balls or use a 40mm spring-loaded scoop. Place on parchment-lined or greased baking sheets.

Press each cookie gently with a fork.

Bake 10–12 minutes until lightly browned.

*Unbleached flour may be substituted when barley flour is unavailable.

Yield: 30

MACADAMIA CHOCOLATE MOUNDS

8 oz	bittersweet chocolate, chopped	227 g
2 Tbsp	butter	30 mL
2	eggs	2
⅔ cup	granulated sugar	150 mL
1 tsp	vanilla	5 mL
3 Tbsp	unbleached or barley flour	45 mL
¼ tsp	baking powder	1 mL
2 cups	toasted macadamia nuts, chopped	500 mL
1 ½ cups	semi-sweet chocolate chips	375 mL

Preheat oven to 350°F (180°C). Line 2 large baking sheets with parchment paper.

In saucepan over low heat, melt chocolate and butter. Stir until smooth. Remove from heat, cool 20 minutes.

In Bosch Universal Kitchen Machine® bowl equipped with cookie paddles and splash ring, beat eggs, sugar and vanilla until thickened and pale yellow in colour.

Add flour, baking powder, melted chocolate, nuts and chocolate chips. Mix well until combined.

Use 39mm spring-loaded scoop to drop dough onto baking sheets 1-inch apart (2.5 cm), 20 per baking sheet.

Bake both baking sheets at the same time on separate racks in preheated oven 8–9 minutes with centres still soft.

Notes: In conventional oven, place baking sheets on separate racks and rotate sheets to opposite racks halfway through baking time.

In convection oven, bake on separate racks at the same time. Do not rotate baking sheets.

Yield: 40

In my opinion, chocolate should be a food group!

CRANBERRY SPELT COOKIES

I met Shar, from Arizona, US, at a BOSCH™ convention in March 1986. We were both BOSCH™ distributors with similar stores. Exchanging recipes, ideas and lots of laughter, we remain very good friends. She gave me this recipe in 1988.

1 cup	butter, softened	250 mL
1 cup	brown sugar	250 mL
½ cup	granulated sugar	125 mL
2	eggs	2
1 tsp	pure vanilla	5 mL
1 cup	spelt flakes, ground in blender	250 mL
⅔ cup	spelt flour	150 mL
¾ cup	whole wheat flour	175 mL
1 tsp	baking powder	5 mL
½ tsp	baking soda	2 mL
½ tsp	salt	2 mL
1 tsp	cinnamon	5 mL
¼ tsp	allspice	1 mL
Pinch	cloves	pinch
1 cup	spelt flakes	250 mL
½ cup	long shred coconut	125 mL
1 cup	dried cranberries	250 mL

Preheat oven to 350°F (180°C).

In Bosch Universal Kitchen Machine® bowl equipped with cookie paddles and splash ring, beat butter, sugars, eggs and vanilla well.

Add dry ingredients and mix on low speed to combine.

Use 39mm spring-loaded scoop to drop dough onto parchment-lined or silicone-lined baking sheets.

Bake 12–14 minutes until golden.

Cool cookies on baking sheets 2 minutes before transferring to cooling rack.

Variation: Add ½ cup (125 mL) sesame seeds or cracked flax seeds.

Yield: 42

Laugh until your face hurts!

PINEAPPLE MACADAMIA TRIANGLES

I created this recipe to enjoy favourite flavours of Hawaii, 1996.

1 cup	unsalted butter, softened	250 mL
⅔ cup	granulated sugar	150 mL
1 tsp	rum extract	5 mL
2 ½ cups	unbleached flour	625 mL
¼ tsp	salt	1 mL
1 cup	macadamia nuts, finely chopped	250 mL
½ cup	dried pineapple, chopped	125 mL

Preheat oven to 350°F (180°C).

Line 10 x 15-inch (25 x 38 cm) jelly roll pan with parchment paper.

In Bosch Universal Kitchen Machine® bowl equipped with cookie paddles and splash ring, beat butter, sugar and extract. Mix in remaining ingredients to form dough.

Press onto parchment paper.

Use a flat dough scraper or pizza wheel to divide pan in quarters across the width and thirds lengthwise. Cut each square into four triangles.

Bake 15 minutes or until lightly golden. Re-score triangles while hot.

Transfer to wire rack to cool.

ICING

1 ½ cups	confectioner's (icing) sugar	375 mL
2 Tbsp	pineapple juice	30 mL

Beat in small bowl until smooth. Spoon icing into pastry bag fitted with small writing tip.

Pipe stripes on each cookie. Let dry before storing.

Yield: 48

These have a shortbread texture and the taste reminds me of Hawaii.

Pineapple Macadamia Triangles

CHOCOLATE NUT COOKIES

1 cup	butter, softened (do not substitute)	250 mL
1 cup	granulated sugar	250 mL
1 cup	brown sugar	250 mL
2	eggs	2
1 tsp	vanilla	5 mL
1 ¾ cups	spelt flour	425 mL
1 tsp	baking powder	5 mL
1 tsp	baking soda	5 mL
½ tsp	salt	2 mL
2 ½ cups	rolled oats	625 mL
½ cup	toasted almonds, chopped	125 mL
½ cup	pecans, chopped	125 mL
½ cup	walnuts, chopped	125 mL
½ cup	toasted cashews, chopped	125 mL
1 ½ cups	semi-sweet chocolate chips	375 mL

Preheat oven to 375°F (190°C).

In Bosch Universal Kitchen Machine® bowl equipped with cookie paddles and splash ring, combine butter, sugars, eggs and vanilla.

Add dry ingredients and mix to combine.

Use 39mm spring-loaded scoop to drop dough onto greased or parchment-lined baking sheets, 12 per sheet.

Bake 9 minutes or until edges are light brown.

Transfer to wire racks to cool.

Yield: 60

Use a food processor or blender to chop nuts and seeds. Pulse to obtain desired size.

DOUBLE-CHIP OATMEAL CHEWS

Tasty and chewy university lunch box cookies, 1975.

1 cup	butter, softened	250 mL
1 cup	granulated sugar	250 mL
1 cup	brown sugar	250 mL
2	eggs	2
1 tsp	vanilla	5 mL
1 ¾ cups	unbleached flour	425 mL
1 tsp	baking soda	5 mL
3 cups	rolled oats	750 mL
1 cup	semi-sweet chocolate chips	250 mL
1 cup	butterscotch chips	250 mL

Preheat oven to 375°F (190°C).

In Bosch Universal Kitchen Machine® bowl equipped with cookie paddles and splash ring, combine butter, sugars, eggs and vanilla.

Add dry ingredients and mix until combined.

Use 39mm spring-loaded scoop to drop dough 2 inches (5 cm) apart onto parchment-lined or silicone-lined baking sheets.

Bake 8–10 minutes until golden. Cool on baking sheets 1 minute.

Transfer to wire racks.

Yield: 50

SPICY MOLASSES COOKIES

½ cup	butter, softened	125 mL
¼ cup	shortening	60 mL
⅓ cup	granulated sugar	75 mL
⅓ cup	brown sugar	75 mL
1	egg yolk	1
½ cup	blackstrap molasses	125 mL
1 tsp	vanilla	5 mL
1 ¾ cups	unbleached flour	425 mL
½ cup	whole wheat flour	125 mL
1 ½ tsp	cinnamon	7 mL
1 tsp	baking soda	5 mL
1 tsp	ginger	5 mL
¼ tsp	allspice	1 mL
¼ tsp	cloves	1 mL

Preheat oven to 375°F (190°C).

In Bosch Universal Kitchen Machine® bowl equipped with cookie paddles and splash ring, combine butter, shortening, sugars, egg yolk, molasses and vanilla.

Add dry ingredients and mix until combined.

Cover and chill dough one hour.

Use 39mm spring-loaded scoop to place dough 2 inches (5 cm) apart on parchment-lined or silicone-lined baking sheets.

Bake 8–10 minutes until lightly brown on bottom.

Cool cookies 1 minute before transferring to wire rack to cool completely.

Variation: Add 2 tablespoons (30 mL) finely chopped crystallised ginger to batter.

Yield: 42

CHEWY CHOCOLATE COOKIES

Tasty and chewy, 1979.

1 ¼ cups	butter, softened	310 mL
1 ½ cups	granulated sugar	375 mL
2	eggs	2
2 tsp	vanilla	10 mL
2 cups	whole wheat flour (less 2 tbsp)	470 mL
¾ cup	Dutch cocoa	175 mL
1 tsp	baking soda	5 mL
½ tsp	salt	2 mL
1 cup	pecans or walnuts, finely chopped	250 mL
½ cup	chocolate chips	125 mL

Preheat oven to 350°F (180°C).

Cream butter and sugar in Bosch Universal Kitchen Machine® bowl equipped with cookie paddles and splash ring.

Add eggs and vanilla and blend well. Add dry ingredients and mix.

Drop onto ungreased baking sheets with 39mm spring-loaded scoop.

Bake 7–8 minutes. Do not overbake.

Cookies will puff during baking and flatten upon cooling while centres remain soft.

Cool on baking sheets 1 minute.

Remove to wire racks to cool completely.

Yield: 54

CHOCOLATE-CHIP OATMEAL COOKIES

Rolled oats and chocolate chips: a staple in our home since we married, 1979.

1 cup	butter, softened	250 mL
¾ cup	brown sugar	175 mL
¼ cup	granulated sugar	60 mL
1 tsp	vanilla	5 mL
1 ½ cups	unbleached flour	375 mL
½ tsp	salt	2 mL
1 tsp	baking soda	5 mL
⅓ cup	boiling water	75 mL
2 cups	rolled oats	500 mL
½ cup	chopped nuts (optional)	125 mL
1 cup	chocolate chips	250 mL

Preheat oven to 350°F (180°C).

In Bosch Universal Kitchen Machine® bowl equipped with batter whips or cookie paddles and splash ring, beat butter, sugars and vanilla.

Add flour and salt. Mix well.

Dissolve baking soda in boiling water. Blend into mixture.

Add rolled oats, nuts and chocolate chips. Pulse momentary switch to combine.

Use a spring-loaded scoop to form 1-inch (2.5 cm) balls and place on parchment-lined or greased baking sheets.

Flatten balls with a fork dipped in cold water.

Bake 10–12 minutes until golden brown.

Cool on wire racks.

CHOCOLATE ALMOND COFFEE COOKIES

½ cup	instant coffee granules	125 mL
2 Tbsp	hot water	30 mL
1 cup	butter, softened	250 mL
1 cup	granulated sugar	250 mL
¾ tsp	baking soda	3 mL
½ tsp	salt	2 mL
2	eggs	2
1 tsp	vanilla	5 mL
2 ⅔ cups	barley flour	650 mL
2 cups	semi-sweet chocolate pieces	500 mL
¾ cup	slivered almonds, toasted	175 mL

Preheat oven to 350°F (180°C).

Dissolve coffee granules in hot water. Set aside.

In Bosch Universal Kitchen Machine® bowl equipped with cookie paddles and splash ring, beat butter, sugar, baking soda and salt.

Beat in coffee mixture, eggs and vanilla.

Add flour, chocolate and almonds. Mix to combine.

Use 39mm spring-loaded scoop to drop cookies 2 inches (5 cm) apart on parchment-lined or greased baking sheets.

Bake 8 minutes.

Let stand 2 minutes. Transfer to wire racks to cool completely.

MARASCHINO COOKIES

1 cup	butter, softened	250 mL
2 cups	granulated sugar	500 mL
2	eggs	2
1 tsp	pure vanilla	5 mL
3 cups	unbleached flour	750 mL
1 tsp	baking soda	5 mL
¾ tsp	salt*	3 mL
1 cup	pecans, chopped	250 mL
1 cup	maraschino cherries, chopped	250 mL

Preheat oven to 375°F (190°C).

In Bosch Universal Kitchen Machine® bowl equipped with cookie paddles and splash ring, cream butter, sugar, eggs and vanilla until frothy.

Add remaining ingredients. Secure splash ring and lid and mix on speed #1 until dry ingredients are incorporated into batter.

Drop onto parchment-lined baking sheets with 39mm spring-loaded scoop, 2 inches (5 cm) apart.

Bake 9–11 minutes until set and lightly browned.

Cookies will flatten and remain chewy.

Freeze well.

*Decrease salt to ½ tsp (2 mL) when using salted butter.

Yield: 54

Cherries are my favourite fruit:
fresh, dried, candied, frozen or canned!!

OLD-FASHIONED MOLASSES DROPS

A university favourite, 1976.

1 cup	shortening	250 mL
½ cup	granulated sugar	125 mL
1	egg	1
1 cup	blackstrap molasses	250 mL
1 tsp	baking soda	5 mL
1 tsp	salt	5 mL
1 tsp	cinnamon	5 mL
½ tsp	cloves	2 mL
3 cups	unbleached flour	750 mL
¾ cup	hot water	175 mL
1 cup	raisins	250 mL

Preheat oven to 375°F (190°C).

In Bosch Universal Kitchen Machine® bowl equipped with cookie paddles and splash ring, cream shortening and sugar.

Add egg and molasses and beat thoroughly.

Add baking soda, salt, cinnamon and cloves.

Alternately mix in flour and water. Add raisins and mix.

Use 39mm spring-loaded scoop to drop dough on greased or parchment-lined baking sheets 2 inches (5 cm) apart.

Bake 11–13 minutes.

Yield: 60

COCONUT MACAROONS

I created this recipe with a soft centre, 1978.

4–5	egg whites	4–5
1–1 ¼ cups	granulated sugar	250–310 mL
¾ tsp	vanilla or almond extract	3 mL
2 ½ cups	shredded coconut	625 mL

Preheat oven to 325°F (165°C).

Beat egg whites until soft peaks form and gradually add sugar to make a moist meringue.

Add flavouring and fold in coconut.

Drop by rounded tablespoons (15 mL) onto baking pans lined with parchment paper.

Decorate with candied cherry bits or finely chopped nuts, if desired.

Bake 20–25 minutes until a delicate brown and inside is not sticky. Test cookies by gently lifting one cookie off the parchment.

Yield: 36

EASY PAN BROWNIES

Adapted from my mom's recipe, 1969.

½ cup	butter	125 mL
2 oz	unsweetened chocolate	57 g
1 cup	granulated sugar	250 mL
½ cup	walnuts, chopped	125 mL
½ cup	unbleached flour	125 mL
1 tsp	vanilla	5 mL
2	eggs	2

Preheat oven to 350°F (180°C).

Melt butter and chocolate in 8 x 8-inch (20 x 20 cm) metal baking pan over medium heat.

Add remaining ingredients and beat with a whisk. Spread evenly.

Bake 25 minutes. Do not overbake.

To serve, sprinkle with confectioner's (icing) sugar, spread with *Chocolate Icing*, or top with fresh fruit, whipping cream and chocolate shavings.

Prep time: less than 5 minutes!

MOCHA BROWNIES

⅔ cup	butter	150 mL
⅓ cup	Dutch cocoa	75 mL
1 tsp	instant coffee granules	5 mL
1 cup	granulated sugar	250 mL
2	eggs	2
1 tsp	vanilla	5 mL
¾ cup	unbleached flour	175 mL
½ cup	semi-sweet chocolate, chopped	125 mL
½ tsp	dried orange zest*	2 mL

Powdered sugar (optional)

Preheat oven to 350°F (180°C).

Melt butter in small saucepan over medium heat. Stir in cocoa powder and coffee granules. Remove from heat and stir in sugar.

Add eggs one at a time, mixing after each addition. Mix in vanilla. Stir in flour, chocolate and orange zest.

Spread batter in greased 8 x 8-inch (20 x 20 cm) pan.

Bake 30 minutes. Cool in pan on wire rack.

Dust with powdered sugar, if desired.

*Use 1 tsp (5 mL) fresh orange zest.

This recipe is easy to mix in the Bosch Universal Kitchen Machine® equipped with the wire whips or in a medium-sized batter bowl.

Yield: 20–24

Try eating squares out of the freezer!! Delicious!

CHOCOLATE PECAN BARS

CRUST

2 cups	freshly ground whole wheat or white wheat flour	500 mL
⅓ cup	granulated sugar	75 mL
⅔ cup	butter, softened	150 mL

FILLING

1 ½ cups	chocolate chips	375 mL
1 ½ cups	corn syrup	375 mL
1 cup	granulated sugar	250 mL
1 ½ tsp	vanilla	7 mL
4	eggs	4
2 ¼ cups	pecans, chopped	560 mL

DRIZZLE

2 oz	chocolate chips	57 g

Preheat oven to 350°F (180°C).

Combine flour, sugar and butter in a bowl. Mix to resemble coarse crumbs.

Press crumbs firmly and evenly into greased 15 x 10-inch (38 x 25 cm) jelly roll pan.

Bake 15 minutes.

Heat chocolate and corn syrup in a saucepan over low heat, stir to melt. Remove from heat.

Stir in sugar, vanilla and eggs until blended. Mix in pecans. Pour filling over hot crust and spread evenly.

Bake 25–30 minutes until filling is firm around edges and slightly soft in the centre.

Cool on wire rack.

Melt chocolate over hot water or microwave on low power 2–3 minutes. Drizzle on bars.

Cool and cut into squares.

WHITE CHOCOLATE BROWNIES

¼ cup	unsalted butter (no substitutes)	60 mL
6 oz	white chocolate, coarsely chopped	170 g
2	eggs	2
½ cup	granulated sugar	125 mL
½ tsp	salt	2 mL
½ tsp	vanilla	2 mL
1 cup	barley flour or unbleached flour	250 mL
½ cup	semi-sweet chocolate pieces	125 mL

Preheat oven to 350°F (180°C).

In small saucepan over low heat melt butter and half the white chocolate, stirring occasionally. Remove pan from heat.

In Bosch Universal Kitchen Machine® bowl equipped with cookie paddles and splash ring, beat eggs until frothy. Add sugar and beat 1–2 minutes until thick.

Add melted chocolate mixture, salt, vanilla and flour. Beat to combine.

Pulse momentary switch to mix remaining chopped white chocolate and chocolate pieces into batter.

Spoon into parchment-lined 8 x 8-inch (20 x 20 cm) pan leaving extra parchment to lift brownies from pan.

Bake 30 minutes or until evenly browned on top.

Cool in pan on wire rack.

Lift brownies by parchment paper edges to a cutting board. Cut into bars.

Yield: 20

White Chocolate Brownies

MATRIMONIAL (DATE) SQUARES

Adapted from my mom's recipe, 1969.

2 cups	unbleached flour	500 mL
1 tsp	baking soda	5 mL
¼ tsp	salt	1 mL
2 cups	brown sugar	500 mL
4 cups	rolled oats	1000 mL
1 ¾ cups	cold butter	425 mL

DATE FILLING

1 ¾ cups	dates, chopped	425 mL
1 ¼ cups	water	310 mL
1 tsp	vanilla	5 mL

Preheat oven to 350°F (180°C).

Cook filling in small pot until dates are soft. Set aside.

Cut butter into dry ingredients to form crumbs resembling small peas.

Press half the crumb mixture in greased 13 x 9 x 2-inch (33 x 23 x 5 cm) pan.

Spread filling evenly over crumb base and top with remaining crumbs. Gently press crumbs with a spatula.

Lightly sprinkle or spray water over cake.

Bake 30 minutes.

Cool completely on wire rack before cutting.

Cooked oatmeal is my idea of a good breakfast. Just eat a row of Matrimonial (Date) Squares! Well, it is oatmeal . . .

Matrimonial (Date) Squares

Matrimonial (Date) Squares

CHEWY CAROB BARS

Adapted from my friend Eileen's recipe, 1984.

1 cup	honey	250 mL
1 ¼ cups	unsweetened carob*	310 mL
¾ cup	sweet carob*	175 mL
1 cup	bran	250 mL
1 cup	unsalted peanuts, chopped	250 mL
½ cup	peanut butter	125 mL
½ cup	raw sunflower seeds, chopped	125 mL

In medium saucepan, melt honey and carob over low heat, stirring constantly.

Add bran, peanuts, peanut butter and sunflower seeds.

Bring to boil over low heat, stirring constantly. Mixture will be very thick.

Pour onto parchment-lined baking sheet. Spread ¼ inch (6 mm) thick.

Cool completely and cut into squares.

Store in layers separated by parchment paper.

Freeze well.

*Any combination of unsweetened or sweet carob, to equal 2 cups (500 mL).

Option: Exchange chocolate chips for carob chips for sweeter tasting bars.

*Carob is a member of the legume family
and may be a chocolate substitute.*

Desserts

LEMON CHEESECAKE

16 oz	cream cheese, softened	454 g
1 ⅓ cups	confectioner's (icing) sugar, sifted	325 mL
1–2 tsp	grated lemon zest	5–10 mL
2 Tbsp	cornstarch	30 mL
2	eggs, room temperature	2
⅓ cup	fresh lemon juice	75 mL

Preheat oven to 325°F (165°C).

Beat cream cheese, sugar, lemon zest, and cornstarch for 1 minute. Beat in eggs one at a time, beating well after each addition. Drizzle lemon juice into creamed mixture and beat on low speed until blended.

Pour batter into prepared *Graham Crumb Crust*. Cover batter with a circle of parchment paper to minimize cracking.

Bake 45–60 minutes until set.

Remove from oven and place on wire rack to cool. Refrigerate 4 hours before removing parchment.

Garnish with blueberries and whipped cream. Serve chilled.

GRAHAM CRUMB CRUST

1 cup	graham crumbs	250 mL	
3 Tbsp	granulated sugar	45 mL	
3 Tbsp	butter, melted	45 mL	
Dash	nutmeg	dash	

Combine all ingredients in small bowl and blend well.

Press into 7-inch (18 cm) springform pan, covering bottom and 1-inch (2.5 cm) up sides.

VARIATION: RASPBERRY CHEESECAKE

Exchange fresh lemon juice with strained, pureed raspberries. Exchange graham crumbs for chocolate crumbs in *Graham Crumb Crust*.

Serve with whole raspberries and whipped cream. Serve chilled.

Yield: 6-8 servings

GERMAN CHEESECAKE

Adapted from my mom's recipe, 1970.

CHEESE FILLING

8 oz	cream cheese, softened	250 g
½ cup	granulated sugar	125 mL
2	eggs	2
3 Tbsp	sour cream	45 mL
3 Tbsp	unbleached flour	45 mL
1 tsp	vanilla	5 mL
½ tsp	lemon extract	2 mL
½ cup	golden raisins	125 mL

BASE

½ cup	butter	125 mL
½ cup	granulated sugar	125 mL
2	eggs	2
1 tsp	vanilla	5 mL
¾ cup	unbleached flour	175 mL
½ tsp	baking powder	2 mL

Preheat oven to 325°F (165°C).

Make filling first. Beat cream cheese and sugar until fluffy. Add eggs, sour cream, flour and flavourings. Beat well. Mix in raisins. Set aside.

For base, beat butter and sugar well. Add remaining ingredients and mix to combine.

Spread base mixture in 10-inch (25 cm) pie pan.

Spread filling evenly over base.

Bake 45 minutes.

Cool on wire rack.

To serve, garnish with whipped cream.

STRAWBERRY COBBLER

Adapted from Rena's recipe, 1978. I lived in her home one summer during university and have wonderful memories of this dessert recipe she shared.

4 cups	strawberries	1000 mL
¼ cup	granulated sugar	60 mL
¼ cup	butter	60 mL
1 cup	granulated sugar	250 mL
1 cup	milk	250 mL
½ tsp	vanilla	2 mL
1 ½ cups	sifted unbleached flour*	375 mL
2 tsp	baking powder	10 mL
½ tsp	salt	2 mL
2 Tbsp	butter	30 mL
1 ½ cups	boiling water	375 mL

Wash, hull and slice strawberries. Add ¼ cup (60 mL) sugar and let stand one hour at room temperature. Stir occasionally.

Preheat oven to 350°F (180°C). Grease 13 x 9 x 2-inch (33 x 23 x 5 cm) pan.

Cream butter and 1 cup (250 mL) sugar. Stir in milk and vanilla. Sift dry ingredients. Stir into creamed mixture to blend. Spread in baking pan.

Sprinkle fruit evenly over batter, dot with butter, and pour boiling water over fruit.

Bake 45–50 minutes until batter rises to the top and forms a browned cake-like layer that springs back when touched gently in the centre.

Serve hot with ice cream or whipped cream.

Note: Do not add ¼ cup (60 mL) sugar when using frozen fruit.

*Exchange unbleached flour with fresh ground whole wheat flour.

BLUEBERRY COBBLER

Adapted from Rena's recipe, 1978.

Exchange blueberries for strawberries. Continue with recipe.

FRUIT CRISP

Adapted from my mom's recipe, 1970.

CRUMB TOPPING

1 cup	butter	250 mL
1 ¼ cups	whole wheat flour	310 mL
1 ½ cups	rolled oats	375 mL
½ cup	wheat germ*	125 mL
2 cups	brown sugar	500 mL
2 ½ tsp	cinnamon	12 mL
2 ½ tsp	nutmeg	12 mL
1 cup	walnuts or pecans, chopped (optional)	250 mL

Preheat oven to 350°F (180°C).

Mix dry ingredients except nuts. Cut in butter to resemble coarse crumbs.

*Increase flour by ½ cup (125 mL) when wheat germ is unavailable.

FRUIT

Mix desired amount of fresh fruit with about 2 Tbsp (30 mL) Ultra Sperse M®*. Arrange in greased casserole or baking pan.

Generously sprinkle crumb topping on fruit. Top with nuts, if desired.

Bake 30–45 minutes until topping is browned and fruit bubbles.

Serve with ice cream or whipped cream.

Note: If using dehydrated fruit, rehydrate in water and drain before adding to recipe.

*Ultra Sperse M® is a commercial thickening agent made from corn. It is gluten-free and may be added to hot or cold liquids, or added to fruit with or without sugar. Available in specialty food stores. May be substituted with ClearJel® or cornstarch.

Store crumb topping in the freezer for quick desserts.

GINGER PEACH CRUMBLE

4 cups	sliced peeled peaches	1000 mL
¼ cup	candied ginger, chopped	60 mL
1 Tbsp	Ultra Sperse M®*	15 mL
¾ cup	rolled oats**	175 mL
½ cup	packed brown sugar	125 mL
¼ cup	fresh ground whole wheat flour	60 mL
1 tsp	cinnamon	5 mL
½ cup	cold butter, cubed	125 mL
½ cup	slivered almonds, (optional)	125 mL

Preheat oven to 350°F (180°C).

In a bowl, toss peaches with ginger and Ultra Sperse M®. Set aside.

Combine rolled oats, sugar, flour and cinnamon in Bosch Universal Kitchen Machine® bowl equipped with wire whips or cookie paddles and lids.

Cut in butter by pulsing momentary switch to resemble coarse crumbs.

Add almonds and pulse to mix.

Divide peach mixture into 6, 1-cup (250 mL) greased baking dishes.

Top evenly with crumbs and place on a baking sheet.

Bake 35–40 minutes until golden brown and fruit is bubbling.

Serve warm with ice cream or whipped cream.

*Ultra Sperse M® is a commercial thickening agent made from corn. It is gluten-free and may be added to hot or cold liquids, or added to fruit with or without sugar. Available in specialty stores. May be substituted with ClearJel® or cornstarch. Ultra Sperse M® and ClearJel®: modified cornstarch that does not break down at high heat. Maintains its thickening powers.

**Exchange rolled oats for rolled barley, spelt, wheat, rye, triticale or Kamut®.

BAVARIAN APPLE TORTE

Adapted from my mom's recipe, 1980.

¾ cup	butter	175 mL
½ cup	granulated sugar	125 mL
½ tsp	clear vanilla	2 mL
1 ½ cups	unbleached flour	375 mL

Preheat oven to 350°F (180°C).

Cream butter, sugar and vanilla. Add flour and mix to form dough.

Spread and press dough in 10-inch (25 cm) springform pan.

Bavarian Apple Torte

FILLING

12 oz	cream cheese, room temperature	340 g
½ cup	granulated sugar	125 mL
2	eggs	2
¾ tsp	clear vanilla	3 mL

Beat cream cheese until soft. Add sugar and cream well. Add eggs and vanilla and beat.

Pour filling mixture over dough.

TOPPING

2 cups	finely sliced apples	500 mL
½ cup	granulated sugar	125 mL
1 tsp	cinnamon	5 mL
⅓ cup	sliced blanched almonds	75 mL

Mix first three ingredients and spoon over cheese mixture.

Sprinkle almonds over filling.

Bake 50–60 minutes until lightly browned.

An apple wedger quickly cuts apples into even-sized wedges. So handy!

Bavarian Apple Torte

CHOCOLATE PECAN TORTE

4	eggs, separated	4
½ cup	granulated sugar	125 mL
⅔ cup	unbleached flour	150 mL
½ tsp	baking soda	2 mL
¼ tsp	salt	1 mL
¾ cup	ground pecans	175 mL
⅓ cup	Dutch cocoa	75 mL
¼ cup	water	60 mL
1 tsp	vanilla	5 mL
¼ cup	granulated sugar	60 mL

Preheat oven to 350°F (180°C).

Grease sides of 2, 9-inch (23 cm) round cake pans. Line bottoms with parchment paper.

Beat egg yolks on high speed. Gradually add ½ cup (125 mL) sugar, beating until mixture is thick and pale in colour.

Combine dry ingredients and add to yolk batter, alternating with water. Mix in vanilla.

Beat egg whites on high speed until foamy. Gradually add ¼ cup (60 mL) sugar until stiff peaks form. Fold into yolk batter. Pour batter into prepared pans.

Bake 16–18 minutes until cake tester comes out clean.

Cool in pans on wire rack 10 minutes. Remove from pans and cool completely.

CHOCOLATE FROSTING

⅓ cup	confectioner's (icing) sugar	75 mL
⅓ cup	Dutch cocoa	75 mL
2 cups	whipping cream	500 mL
1 ½ tsp	vanilla	7 mL

Beat ingredients on low speed until blended. Beat on high speed until stiff peaks form.

Split cake layers in half horizontally to make 4 layers. Place 1 layer on serving plate. Spread with ¾ cup (175 mL) *Chocolate Frosting*. Repeat for remaining layers. Spread remaining frosting on torte top and sides.

GINGERBREAD TORTE

½ cup	shortening	125 mL
½ cup	brown sugar	125 mL
1	egg	1
⅔ cup	blackstrap molasses	150 mL
1 cup	boiling water	250 mL
2 cups	unbleached flour	500 mL
1 ½ tsp	baking soda	7 mL
1 tsp	salt	5 mL
1 ½ tsp	ginger	7 mL
1 tsp	cinnamon	5 mL
½ tsp	cloves	2 mL

Preheat oven to 375°F (190°C).

In Bosch Universal Kitchen Machine® bowl equipped with wire whips and splash ring, beat shortening, brown sugar and egg.

Add molasses and water. Mix well.

Add dry ingredients. Cover and beat until smooth.

Pour into 2, greased 9-inch (23 cm) cake pans, dividing evenly.

Bake 30–35 minutes or until cake tester comes out clean.

Cool 10 minutes before removing from pans.

Cool completely on wire rack.

FILLING

2 cups	whipping cream	500 mL
2 Tbsp	confectioner's (icing) sugar	30 mL

Beat cream and sugar until stiff peaks form.

Split cake layers in half horizontally to make 4 layers. Place 1 layer on serving plate and spread with ½ cup (125 mL) filling. Repeat for remaining layers. Spread remaining filling on torte top and sides.

Decorate as desired.

Optional Fillings: Chocolate ganache or whipped cream with cinnamon.

The smell of Christmas any time of the year!

LEMON POPPY SEED TORTE

1 cup	whole milk*	250 mL
1 Tbsp	lemon juice	15 mL
1 Tbsp	finely grated lemon zest	15 mL
⅓ cup	poppy seeds	75 mL
1 cup	butter	250 mL
1 cup	granulated sugar	250 mL
1 cup	confectioner's (icing) sugar	250 mL
3	egg yolks	3
1 tsp	vanilla	5 mL
2 cups	unbleached flour	500 mL
1 tsp	baking soda	5 mL
½ tsp	salt	2 mL
3	egg whites, room temperature	3

Preheat oven to 350°F (180°C).

Line half sheet baking pan with parchment paper, extending 2 inches over long sides.

Heat milk in small saucepan until very hot and bubbles appear around edge of pan. Remove from heat. Stir in lemon juice, lemon zest and poppy seeds. Let stand 15 minutes or until room temperature.

Beat butter in large bowl or Bosch Universal Kitchen Machine® bowl equipped with wire whips, until creamy and light colour. Add sugars and beat well. Beat in egg yolks and vanilla.

In small bowl, mix flour, baking soda and salt. Add to butter mixture in 3 parts, alternating with poppy seed mixture.

Beat egg whites in small bowl until stiff peaks form. Gently fold ½ the egg whites into batter by pulsing momentary switch. Fold in remaining whites until no white streaks remain.

Spread batter evenly in prepared pan.

Bake 20 minutes until cake tester inserted in cake centre comes out clean.

Cool cake completely in baking sheet on wire rack. Invert cake onto cutting board and remove parchment paper. Cut cake into 3 rectangles.

Continue with *Lemon Buttercream Icing* (next page).

*Exchange 3 Tbsp (45 mL) whole milk powder whisked into water to measure 1 cup (250 mL) if liquid whole milk is unavailable.

LEMON POPPY SEED TORTE (Continued . . .)

LEMON BUTTERCREAM ICING

1 cup	butter, softened	250 mL
9 cups	confectioner's (icing) sugar	2250 mL
3–6 Tbsp	lemon juice	45–90 mL
1 ½ tsp	finely grated lemon zest	7 mL

In medium bowl, beat butter and sugar on low speed. Add 3 Tbsp (45 mL) lemon juice and zest. Beat well.

Gradually beat in additional lemon juice to make icing smooth and spreadable.

TO ASSEMBLE TORTE

Place one cake piece on cake board or serving plate. Spread with ¾ cup (175 mL) icing.

Repeat with second and third cake pieces.

Ice top and sides of cake with thin icing layer.

Spoon remaining icing into large piping bag fitted with star tip.

Pipe small stars on cake top and sides.

Chill several hours until firm before slicing.

Yield: 24 slices

Lemons and poppy seeds . . . so good!

HAZELNUT TORTE

Adapted from my friend Brenda's recipe, 1989.

4	eggs	4
¾ cup	granulated sugar	175 mL
1 cup	hazelnuts (filberts)*	250 mL
2 ½ tsp	baking powder	12 mL
2 Tbsp	whole wheat flour**	30 mL

Preheat oven to 350°F (180°C).

Grease and flour 2, 8-inch (20 cm) pans, or grease pan sides and line bottoms with parchment.

Pour eggs and sugar in blender, cover and process. Add hazelnuts and baking powder. Continue processing on high speed until nuts are very finely ground.

Add flour and process until mixed well. Pour batter into prepared pans.

Bake 20 minutes or until cake tester comes out clean.

Cool cakes. Remove cakes from pans and layer with whipped cream and fruit. Decorate with sliced nuts to match nuts in torte.

*Exchange hazelnuts for almonds or pecans.

**Flour measurement is correct. Ground nuts replace part of the flour.

Prep time: less than 5 minutes!

WHOLE WHEAT FLAN DESSERT

Adapted from my mom's recipe, 1988.

2	eggs, separated	2
2 Tbsp	cold water	30 mL
½ cup	granulated sugar	125 mL
¾ cup	fresh ground whole wheat flour	175 mL
½ tsp	salt	2 mL
1 tsp	baking powder	5 mL
¼ tsp	vanilla	1 mL
¼ tsp	lemon extract	1 mL

Preheat oven to 400°F (200°C).

In Bosch Universal Kitchen Machine® bowl equipped with wire whips and splash ring, beat egg yolks until fluffy and lemon-coloured.

Add cold water and beat well. Gradually beat in sugar.

Add dry ingredients and flavourings. Mix.

Beat egg whites in separate bowl. Fold into yolk mixture by pulsing momentary switch. Pour into greased, floured flan pan.

Bake 13 minutes.

FLAN FILLING

4 cups	chopped rhubarb	1000 mL
¼ cup	water	60 mL
1 ½ cups	granulated sugar	375 mL
2 Tbsp	cornstarch	30 mL
¼ cup	water	60 mL
4 cups	chopped strawberries	1000 mL

Simmer rhubarb, ¼ cup (60 mL) water and sugar 20–30 minutes in a saucepan.

Combine cornstarch in ¼ cup (60 mL) water. Stir into rhubarb and continue cooking until thickened. Add strawberries and mix.

Spread on flan base.

Serve with ice cream or dollop of whipped cream.

CREAM PUFFS (PROFITEROLES)

Adapted from Anne's recipe, a university roommate, 1976.

1 cup	water	250 mL
¼ tsp	salt	1 mL
½ cup	butter	125 mL
1 ¼ cups	sifted unbleached flour	310 mL
3 – 4	eggs, room temperature	3–4

Whipped cream, sweetened
Confectioner's (icing) sugar

Preheat oven to 400°F (200°C). Sift flour before measuring.

Heat water, salt and butter in a 4-quart (4 litre) saucepan over medium heat until butter melts and water begin to boil. Add flour all at once, beating constantly with a wooden spoon until thick and smooth.

Remove from heat and continue beating until dough forms a smooth, glossy ball. Add eggs one at a time, beating until smooth after each addition. Dough should be soft, not runny, and stiff enough to hold a plump, round mound. The fourth egg may not be required.

Use a spoon or pastry bag with large tip, place dough 2 inches (5 cm) apart onto parchment-lined baking sheets.

Bake immediately for 25 minutes.

When cool, cut top of cream puff to lift a cap. Fill with whipped cream.

To serve, dust with confectioner's (icing) sugar, fill with whipped cream, *Blender Chocolate Mousse* (next page), or drizzle with melted chocolate.

Yield: 20

Cream Puffs (Profiteroles)

BLENDER CHOCOLATE MOUSSE

Adapted from Anne's recipe, a university roommate, 1975.

3	eggs	3
2 tsp	vanilla	10 mL
1 tsp	orange extract	5 mL
1 cup	Dutch cocoa	250 mL
⅔ cup	granulated sugar	150 mL
⅔ cup	butter	150 mL
1 ¼ cups	milk	310 mL

Place eggs and flavourings in blender jar. Cover and blend on high speed one minute.

In a saucepan, combine cocoa and sugar. Add butter and milk. Cook over medium heat, stirring constantly until butter melts and mixture is hot.

Turn blender speed to high and slowly pour hot mixture through blender funnel. Continue blending one minute.

Pour into serving dishes. Cover and chill several hours.

Serve with sweetened whipped cream.

Decorate with shaved chocolate, strawberries, etc.

Yield: 6

STRAWBERRY CHEESECAKE MOUSSE

8 oz	cream cheese, softened and cubed	250 g
2 cups	sliced strawberries	500 mL
½ cup	confectioner's (icing) sugar	125 mL
½ tsp	vanilla	2 mL
1 ½ cups	whipping cream, whipped	375 mL

Process cream cheese, strawberries, sugar and vanilla in food processor until smooth.

Transfer to large bowl. Fold in whipped cream.

Spoon into small dessert dishes or wine glasses. Refrigerate to set.

To serve, garnish with additional whipped cream, sliced strawberries or chocolate curls.

Prep time: less than 5 minutes!

Blender Chocolate Mousse

Muffins

ANYTIME LOW-FAT MUFFINS

I met Shar, from Arizona, US, at a BOSCH™ convention in March 1986. We were both BOSCH™ distributors with similar stores. Exchanging recipes, ideas and lots of laughter, we remain very good friends. She gave me this versatile recipe in 1988.

1 cup	large flaked oatmeal	250 mL
1 cup	boiling water	250 mL
¾ cup	canola or vegetable oil	175 mL
1 cup	honey	250 mL
2 cups	buttermilk, yogurt or skim milk	500 mL
3	eggs, or 6 egg whites	3
2 cups	fresh ground whole wheat pastry flour*	500 mL
1 ½ cups	unbleached flour	375 mL
1 cup	oat bran	250 mL
1 ½ cups	wheat bran	375 mL
1 Tbsp	baking soda	15 mL
1 Tbsp	baking powder	15 mL
2 tsp	salt	10 mL

Preheat oven to 350°F (180°C).

Combine oat flakes and boiling water. Let stand to absorb water.

Combine oat flake mixture and remaining ingredients in Bosch Universal Kitchen Machine® bowl equipped with batter whisks or cookie paddles and lids. Do not overmix.

Fill greased muffin pans ¾ full.

Bake 20 minutes or until springy to touch.

Cool 5 minutes in pans before removing to wire racks.

Option: Exchange 1 cup (250 mL) whole wheat pastry flour with 1 cup (250 mL) barley flour.

*Grind soft white wheat kernels to obtain fresh whole wheat pastry flour.

Yield: 36

Anytime Low-Fat Muffins
(Apricot Variation)

ANYTIME LOW-FAT MUFFIN VARIATIONS
(Shar's Recipes, 1988)

APRICOT MUFFINS

Add 1 ½ cups (375 mL) chopped dried apricots, 1 cup (250 mL) sliced or slivered almonds and 2 tsp (10 mL) almond extract to basic recipe.

CRANBERRY WALNUT MUFFINS

Add 2 cups (500 mL) dried cranberries, 1 cup (250 mL) chopped walnuts and 1 tsp (5 mL) orange extract to basic recipe.

DATE MUFFINS

Add 1, 14-oz can (398 mL) pumpkin, 2 cups (500 mL) chopped dates and 2 tsp (10 mL) maple extract to basic recipe.

RAISIN OR CURRANT MUFFINS

Add 2 cups (500 mL) raisins or currants and 2 tsp (10 mL) vanilla to basic recipe.

ZUCCHINI MUFFINS

Add 1 ½ cups (375 mL) shredded zucchini and 1 cup (250 mL) chopped walnuts or coconut to basic recipe.

Anytime Low-Fat Muffins
(Apricot Variation)

WHOLE WHEAT MUFFINS

Adapted from my friend Eileen's recipe, 1984.

¼ cup	butter, softened	60 mL
¼ cup	granulated sugar	60 mL
1	egg	1
2 cups	whole wheat flour	500 mL
1 Tbsp	baking powder	15 mL
½ tsp	salt	2 mL
1 cup	milk	250 mL

Preheat oven to 375°F (190°C).

Mix butter, sugar and egg in a Bosch Universal Kitchen Machine® bowl equipped with wire whips and splash ring. Add dry ingredients and milk. Mix to combine.

Fill greased muffin tins ¾ full.

Bake 20–25 minutes.

Yield: 12

WHOLE WHEAT MUFFIN VARIATIONS

APPLE CINNAMON MUFFINS

Add 1 ½ cups (375 mL) chopped apples and 2 tsp (10 mL) cinnamon to basic recipe.

BLUEBERRY MUFFINS

Add 1 ½ cups (375 mL) fresh blueberries, 2 tsp (10 mL) lemon juice and 1 tsp (5 mL) grated lemon zest to basic recipe.

COCONUT MUFFINS

Add 1 tsp (5 mL) coconut extract and 1 cup (250 mL) raw or toasted unsweetened coconut to basic recipe.

WHOLE WHEAT MUFFIN VARIATIONS (Continued . . .)

LEMON POPPY SEED MUFFINS

Add grated zest of 1 lemon, ¼ cup (60 mL) poppy seeds and 1 tsp (5 mL) almond extract to basic recipe.

PEACH AND RASPBERRY MUFFINS

Add ¾ cup (175 mL) chopped peaches and ¾ cup (175 mL) raspberries to basic recipe. Sprinkle a mixture of brown sugar and cinnamon on muffin tops before baking.

POLYNESIAN MUFFINS

Add 1 ½ cups (375 mL) drained crushed pineapple, ¼ cup (60 mL) coconut and ¼ tsp (1 mL) nutmeg to basic recipe.

SUNSHINE MUFFINS

Add 1 ½ cups (375 mL) chopped citrus fruits and 1 tsp (5 mL) vanilla or almond extract to basic recipe.

SURPRISE MUFFINS

Fill greased muffin tins ½ full with batter. Top batter with 1 Tbsp (15 mL) jam. Fill muffin cups ¾ full with remaining batter.

BACON TOMATO CHEESE MUFFINS

Add ¼ cup (60 mL) bacon bits, 1 chopped fresh tomato and 1 cup (250 mL) shredded cheese to basic recipe.

CORN MUFFINS

Exchange cornmeal for flour and add 1 ½ cups (375 mL) kernel corn to basic recipe.

ONION CHEDDAR MUFFINS

Add ½ cup (125 mL) finely chopped onion, 1 cup (250 mL) shredded cheddar cheese and ¼ cup (60 mL) parsley to basic recipe.

APPLESAUCE SPICE MUFFINS

Growing crabapples in our backyard led me to create this recipe, 1980.

½ cup	butter, softened	125 mL
½ cup	granulated sugar	125 mL
¼ cup	packed brown sugar	60 mL
1	egg	1
1 tsp	pure vanilla	5 mL
1 cup	unsweetened applesauce	250 mL
½ cup	durum flour*	125 mL
½ cup	unbleached flour (+ ⅛ cup)	155 mL
¾ cup	graham cracker crumbs	175 mL
1 tsp	baking soda	5 mL
1 ½ tsp	cinnamon	7 mL
¼ tsp	allspice	1 mL
½ cup	chopped walnuts	125 mL
½ cup	raisins	125 mL

Preheat oven to 350°F (180°C).

In Bosch Universal Kitchen Machine® bowl equipped with batter whips or cookie paddles and splash ring, cream butter, sugars, egg and vanilla.

Add applesauce and mix. Add dry ingredients and lids. Mix to combine.

Fill greased or paper-lined muffin cups ¾ full.

Bake 20–25 minutes until browned.

Cool 5 minutes before removing from pans. Cool on wire racks.

*Exchange with whole wheat flour.

Yield: 12

*Durum, a soft wheat grown specially for pasta,
grinds into excellent flour for muffins!*

BLUEBERRY MUFFINS

A favourite of mine since 1979.

¼ cup	butter, softened	60 mL
¾ cup	granulated sugar	175 mL
1	egg	1
1 ½ cups	unbleached flour	375 mL
½ tsp	salt	2 mL
2 tsp	baking powder	10 mL
½ cup	milk	125 mL
1 cup	blueberries, fresh or frozen	250 mL

Preheat oven to 375°F (190°C).

Beat butter, sugar and egg. Mix dry ingredients together.

Add dry ingredients to batter alternately with milk. Mix to combine.

Fold in blueberries.

Bake 15–20 minutes.

Cool on wire rack.

Option: Add dried or fresh lemon zest.

Prep time: less than 5 minutes!

Yield: 12

Blueberries and lemon:
a fabulous combination!

BANANA MUFFINS

Adapted from Rena's recipe, 1978. I lived in her home one summer during university and have wonderful memories of the recipes and laughter we shared.

½ cup	canola or vegetable oil	125 mL
¾ cup	granulated sugar	175 mL
1	egg	1
1 tsp	vanilla	5 mL
2	ripe bananas	2
Pinch	salt	pinch
1 ½ cups	unbleached flour	375 mL
¼ cup	water, boiling	60 mL
1 tsp	baking soda	5 mL

Preheat oven to 375°F (190°C).

Beat oil, sugar, egg, vanilla and bananas. Add salt and flour. Mix.

Dissolve baking soda in water. Add soda water to batter and mix well.

Bake 20–25 minutes.

Cool on wire racks. Ice before serving.

Prep time: less than 5 minutes!

ICING

1 cup	confectioner's (icing) sugar	250 mL
1 Tbsp	butter	15 mL
1 Tbsp	milk	15 mL
1 tsp	vanilla	5 mL

Mix well in small bowl. Ice cooled muffins.

Yield: 18

Chocolate chips: a favourite addition to any muffin recipe!

Banana Muffins

CITRUS PECAN MUFFINS

1 cup	boiling water	250 mL
¼ cup	butter	60 mL
¼ cup	candied citrus peel	60 mL
1 ½ cups	wheat or oat bran	375 mL
¾ cup	milk	175 mL
1	egg	1
½ cup	brown sugar	125 mL
2 cups	whole wheat flour	500 mL
1 Tbsp	baking powder	15 mL
½ cup	chopped pecans	125 mL
½ tsp	salt	2 mL

Preheat oven to 350°F (180°C).

Pour boiling water over butter, citrus peel and bran in Bosch Universal Kitchen Machine®
bowl equipped with wire whips or batter whips and splash ring. Mix until butter melts.
Cool.

Add milk, egg and sugar. Mix gently.

Add remaining ingredients and mix well.

Fill greased muffins pans ⅔ full.

Bake 20 minutes. Serve with *Honey Butter*.

HONEY BUTTER

¼ cup	butter, softened	60 mL
2 Tbsp	liquid honey	30 mL
1 Tbsp	citrus peel (zest)	15 mL

Beat well and serve on *Citrus Pecan Muffins*.

Yield: 18

Wheat bran and oat bran are interchangeable.

CRANBERRY ORANGE MUFFINS

1 cup	dried cranberries	250 mL
2 cups	unbleached flour	500 mL
½ cup	granulated sugar	125 mL
1 tsp	baking powder	5 mL
½ tsp	baking soda	2 mL
½ tsp	salt	2 mL
1 Tbsp	grated orange rind (zest)	15 mL
1	egg	1
¼ cup	canola or vegetable oil	60 mL
¾ cup	milk	175 mL
1 tsp	vanilla	5 mL

Preheat oven to 350°F (180°C).

Stir cranberries into dry ingredients.

Combine egg, oil, milk and vanilla in Bosch Universal Kitchen Machine® bowl equipped with wire whips and splash ring.

Add dry ingredients and cranberries. Pulse momentary switch to combine.

Fill muffin cups ¾ full.

Bake 15–20 minutes.

Prep time: less than 5 minutes!

Yield: 12

Zest oranges on parchment paper to dry. Use as desired.

LEMON POPPY SEED MUFFINS

2 cups	rolled oats	500 mL
2 cups	hot water	500 mL
1 cup	canola or vegetable oil*	250 mL
1 ½ cups	honey	375 mL
4 cups	buttermilk	1000 mL
4	eggs, or 8 egg whites	4
5 cups	fresh ground whole wheat pastry flour	1250 mL
2 cups	oat bran	500 mL
3 cups	wheat bran	750 mL
5 tsp	baking soda	25 mL
1 Tbsp	baking powder	15 mL
1 tsp	salt	5 mL
½ cup	poppy seeds	125 mL
Zest	2 lemons	zest

Preheat oven to 350°F (180°C). Juice and zest 2 lemons.

Mix rolled oats and hot water in Bosch Universal Kitchen Machine® bowl equipped with wire whips, batter whips or cookie paddles and splash ring. Let stand 10 minutes.

Add oil, honey, buttermilk and eggs and mix well. Add remaining ingredients and mix to combine.

Fill greased muffin cups ⅔ full.

Bake 20–25 minutes.

*½ cup (125 mL) applesauce may be substituted for ½ cup (125 mL) oil.

GLAZE

½ cup	lemon juice	125 mL
½ cup	granulated sugar	125 mL

Mix well. Dip tops of hot baked muffins in glaze and cool on wire racks.

Yield: 48

OAT BRAN MUFFINS

I created this recipe for university lunches, 1975.

1	egg	1
½ cup	brown sugar	125 mL
¼ cup	honey	60 mL
1 cup	milk	250 mL
½ tsp	salt	2 mL
1 tsp	vanilla	5 mL
¼ cup	canola or vegetable oil	60 mL
1 ¼ cups	unbleached flour	310 mL
¾ cup	oat bran	175 mL
2 tsp	baking powder	10 mL
¼ tsp	cinnamon	1 mL

Preheat oven to 400°F (200°C).

Mix egg, sugar, honey, milk, salt, vanilla and oil in Bosch Universal Kitchen Machine® bowl equipped with wire whips and splash ring.

Add dry ingredients and mix well.

Fill greased muffin cups ⅔ full.

Bake 20–22 minutes.

Cool on wire rack.

Option: Add chocolate chips.

Yield: 12

Chocolate baking chips are delicious in muffins.

HEALTHY BRAN MUFFINS

A muffin with excellent texture, adapted in 1988. Use ingredients in your cupboard.

2	eggs	2
¾ cup	milk	175 mL
⅓ cup	honey	75 mL
¼ cup	canola or vegetable oil	60 mL
1 cup	fresh ground whole wheat flour	250 mL
1 cup	wheat bran	250 mL
2 tsp	baking powder	10 mL
1 tsp	cinnamon	5 mL
½ tsp	salt	2 mL
¼ tsp	nutmeg	1 mL
1 tsp	dried orange zest (peel)	5 mL
⅓ cup	chopped nuts	75 mL
½ cup	sunflower seeds (optional)	125 mL
¼ cup	sesame seeds	60 mL
½ cup	flax seeds, cracked	125 mL
¼ cup	pumpkin seeds (optional)	60 mL
¼ cup	millet	60 mL
⅓ cup	shredded coconut, unsweetened	75 mL
½ cup	dried apricots or pitted diced dates	125 mL
½ cup	raisins or cranberries	125 mL

Preheat oven to 375°F (190°C).

Mix eggs, milk, honey and oil in Bosch Universal Kitchen Machine® bowl equipped with wire whips, batter whips or cookie paddles and lids.

Add remaining ingredients and mix to combine.

Store batter in refrigerator up to 10 days.

Fill greased muffin cups ¾ full.

Bake 15–20 minutes.

Yield: 18–20

Not your everyday bran muffin!

Healthy Bran Muffins

ORANGE AND DATE MUFFINS

2	oranges (unpeeled) chopped	2
1 cup	orange juice	250 mL
½ cup	canola or vegetable oil	125 mL
2	eggs	2
1 cup	pitted dates	250 mL
2 cups	whole wheat flour	500 mL
1 cup	bran	250 mL
2 tsp	baking powder	10 mL
2 tsp	baking soda	10 mL
½ tsp	salt	2 mL
¾ cup	granulated sugar	175 mL

Preheat oven to 375°F (190°C).

In a blender, combine oranges, juice, oil, eggs and dates until well blended.

In a separate bowl combine flour, bran, baking powder, baking soda, salt and sugar.

Add orange mixture to dry ingredients. Mix well.

Fill greased muffin tins ⅔ full.

Bake 20 minutes.

Cool on wire rack.

Yield: 18

STRAWBERRY RHUBARB MUFFINS

¾ cup	chopped rhubarb	175 mL
¼ cup	granulated sugar	60 mL
1 cup	strawberry yogurt*	250 mL
½ cup	canola or vegetable oil	125 mL
¾ cup	brown sugar	175 mL
1	egg	1
1 cup	rolled oats	250 mL
1 cup	whole wheat flour	250 mL
1 tsp	salt	5 mL
½ tsp	baking soda	2 mL
1 tsp	baking powder	5 mL
1 tsp	cinnamon	5 mL
1 cup	wheat bran	250 mL
½ cup	sliced strawberries	125 mL

Preheat oven to 400°F (200°C).

In small bowl, mix rhubarb and granulated sugar.

Combine yogurt, oil, brown sugar and egg in Bosch Universal Kitchen Machine® bowl equipped with wire whips and splash ring.

Add dry ingredients, rhubarb and strawberries. Pulse momentary switch to combine.

Fill greased muffin cups ¾ full.

Bake 20 minutes.

Cool on wire rack.

*Natural or vanilla yogurt may be exchanged.

Yield: 12

PINEAPPLE CARROT MUFFINS

My university friend Dawn's recipe, 1975. So easy and extremely moist!

2 cups	granulated sugar	500 mL
3 cups	unbleached flour*	750 mL
2 tsp	baking powder	10 mL
2 tsp	baking soda	10 mL
1 tsp	salt	5 mL
2 tsp	cinnamon	10 mL
4	eggs	4
1 ⅓ cups	canola or vegetable oil	325 mL
1, 14-oz can	crushed pineapple, with juice	398 mL
2 cups	grated carrots	500 mL
2 tsp	vanilla	10 mL

Preheat oven to 325°F (165°C).

Mix first six ingredients together.

Add remaining ingredients and beat well.

Bake 25 minutes or until springy to touch.

Cool on wire rack.

*Exchange part of flour with fresh ground whole wheat flour.

Yield: 48

Pineapple Carrot Muffins

Pies

PIE CRUST MIX

Adapted from my mom's recipe, 1972.

5 cups	soft white wheat pastry flour* or unbleached flour	1250 mL
1 tsp	salt	5 mL
1 lb	cold lard or shortening	454 g

Measure flour and salt into Bosch Universal Kitchen Machine® bowl equipped with wire whips. Cube cold lard or shortening. Add to flour. Position splash ring and lid on bowl.

Pulse momentary switch until mixture resembles coarse meal.

Store pastry crumbs in refrigerator or freezer until ready to use. Prepared crumbs make for an amazingly easy impromptu pie!

*Grind 3 cups (750 mL) soft white wheat kernels in NutriMill Flour Mill®. Measure after milling.

If Bosch Universal Kitchen Machine® is not available, use pastry blender and large mixing bowl.

Yield: 8 single crusts or 4 double crust pies

PIE CRUST

Single Crust Pie	Mix	Ice Water
8 inch (20 cm)	1 ¼ cups (310 mL)	3 Tablespoons (45 mL)
9 inch (23 cm)	1 ½ cups (375 mL)	4 Tablespoons (60 mL)
10 inch (25 cm)	1 ¾ cups (425 mL)	5 Tablespoons (75 mL)

To prepare pastry, measure cold crumbs into medium bowl and add cold water, stir with a fork to form a ball. Do not overmix or pastry will be tough.

Roll pastry on lightly floured surface to desired thickness and diameter. Gently ease pastry into pie pan and trim excess pastry.

Single crust pie shells: gently prick bottom and sides of pastry shell with fork or docker to prevent bubbles while baking.

Bake in preheated 400°F (200°C) oven 8–10 minutes or until lightly brown. Cool before filling.

Double crust pies: Fill unbaked pastry shell according to recipe. Top with pastry. Gently slit steam holes in crust and trim excess pastry. Bake according to recipe.

A time-saver when visitors arrive in the driveway!!

Pie Crust Mix

BARB'S BUTTER TARTS

Adapted from my mom's recipe, 1972.

2	eggs	2
1 cup	granulated sugar	250 mL
⅓ cup	butter	75 mL
¼ cup	half & half cream	60 mL
1 tsp	vanilla	5 mL
1 cup	dried cranberries	250 mL
½ cup	chopped pecans	125 mL

Preheat oven to 375°F (190°C).

In medium saucepan, beat eggs.

Add remaining ingredients except nuts. Boil 3 minutes on medium heat, stirring constantly.

Stir in nuts. Fill unbaked tart shells.

Bake 15 minutes.

Yield: 20

Be kind, giving and forgiving!

Barb's Butter Tarts

COCONUT CREAM PIE

Adapted from my mom's recipe, 1972.

1	9-inch (23 cm) baked pie shell	1

FILLING

3 Tbsp	flour	45 mL
1 Tbsp	cornstarch	15 mL
½ cup	sugar	125 mL
¼ tsp	salt	1 mL
1 cup	milk	250 mL
1 cup	half and half cream	250 mL
2	egg yolks, beaten	2
1 tsp	vanilla	5 mL
¼ cup	shredded coconut	60 mL

Combine flour, cornstarch, sugar and salt in medium saucepan.

In 4-cup (1000 mL) measure, combine milk, cream and yolks. Add to dry ingredients in saucepan.

Cook over low heat until thick, stirring constantly. Add vanilla and coconut. Stir to mix. Cool.

Pour filling into cooled crust.

Sprinkle ½ cup (125 mL) shredded coconut or top with whipped cream and toasted coconut.

BANANA CREAM PIE

Adapted from my mom's recipe, 1972.

Spread 2 sliced bananas in baked pie shell. Prepare cooked filling without coconut and pour over bananas. Cool.

Serve with whipped cream and banana slices.

LEMON MERINGUE PIE

Adapted from my mom's recipe, 1972.

½ cup	water	125 mL
¾ cup	granulated sugar	175 mL
5 Tbsp	cornstarch	75 mL
2	egg yolks	2
1 Tbsp	butter	15 mL
6 Tbsp	lemon juice	90 mL
Pinch	salt	pinch
1 cup	milk or water	250 mL
1 Tbsp	lemon zest	15 mL

Mix all ingredients in blender. Pour into heavy saucepan and cook until thickened, over medium heat, stirring constantly.

Pour into baked 9-inch (23 cm) pie shell and cool 5 minutes. Top with meringue.

MERINGUE

3	egg whites	3
¼ tsp	cream of tartar	1 mL
6 Tbsp	confectioner's (icing) sugar	90 mL
½ tsp	vanilla	2 mL

Preheat oven to 325°F (165°C).

Whip egg whites and cream of tartar until soft peaks form.

Add sugar and vanilla. Continue whipping until stiff peaks form.

Spoon meringue over filling. Gently spread to pastry edge to seal and prevent shrinking. Make peaks with a spatula.

Bake 10–12 minutes or until meringue is golden brown.

Chill before serving.

IMPOSSIBLE PIE

Adapted from my friend Fran's recipe, 1988.

4	eggs	4
½ cup	butter, softened	125 mL
½ cup	unbleached flour	125 mL
2 cups	milk	500 mL
1 cup	granulated sugar	250 mL
1 cup	medium coconut	250 mL
2 tsp	vanilla	10 mL

Preheat oven to 350°F (180°C).

Blend all ingredients in blender until well mixed.

Pour into greased 10-inch (25 cm) pie pan. No pastry required.

Bake 1 hour or until centre tests firm.

Quick and easy. Refreshing coconut taste and texture.

Enjoy!

Prep time: less than 5 minutes!

Impossible Pie

EGG WHITE STAGES

1. FROTHY

Lightly beaten egg whites look bubbly and fluid. At this stage add cream of tartar to stabilise whites, such as a soufflé.

2. SOFT PEAKS

Whites have moist, shiny, small bubbles. When beaters are lifted, peaks form, but tips fold over. The correct stage to fold whites into egg yolk mixture, such as a soufflé.

3. STIFF PEAKS

Whites have lost their sheen. When beaters are lifted, tips stand upright in short, distinct peaks. Do not beat whites beyond this point. The correct stage for meringue.

4. OVERBEATEN

Whites appear dull, dry, and curdled. This unstable dry foam collapses immediately and will be lumpy if added to other ingredients. Not correctable. Start over.

Christmas Treats

FRUITCAKES
CAKES
COOKIES
TARTS
BARS
FUDGE
BALLS
NUTS
FRUIT BREAD
PUDDING

Christmas is all about love.
My favourite time of the year!!

LIGHT FRUITCAKE

Adapted from my mom's recipe, 1972.

1 lb	candied cherries, halved	454 g
2 lbs	deluxe fruit mix*	908 g
2 lbs	sultana raisins	908 g
½ lb	citron peel	227 g
1 cup	mixed glazed fruit	250 mL
1 cup	slivered blanched almonds	250 mL
2 cups	fresh ground whole wheat or unbleached flour	500 mL
3 cups	unbleached flour	750 mL
½ tsp	salt	2 mL
2 tsp	baking powder	10 mL
1 lb	butter, softened	454 g
2 cups	granulated sugar	500 mL
6	eggs	6
1 tsp	vanilla	5 mL
1 tsp	almond extract	5 mL

Preheat oven to 275°F (135°C).

Chop candied cherries and deluxe fruit, place in large bowl. Add raisins, citron, mixed glazed fruit and almonds, dredging with 2 cups (500 mL) whole wheat flour. Mix remaining 3 cups (750 mL) flour with salt and baking powder in a small bowl.

In Bosch Universal Kitchen Machine® bowl equipped with wire whips*, cream butter and sugar. Add eggs, vanilla and extract. Beat well.

Exchange wire whips for dough hook. Pour dry ingredients into mixing bowl. Add fruit and nuts, cover and mix to combine.

Bake in parchment-lined pans until cake tester comes out clean.

Baking times: 4 x 4-inch (10 x 10 cm) cake – 2 ½–3 hours
6 x 6-inch (15 x 15 cm) cake – 3 ½–4 hours
8 x 8-inch (20 x 20 cm) cake – 4 ½–5 hours
8 ½ x 4 ½ x 3-inch (21 x 11 x 8 cm) pans – 2 ½–2 ¾ hours

Cool in pans 15 minutes. Lift cakes onto wire racks to cool completely. Remove parchment. Wrap well. Inspect occasionally. Season 4–6 weeks.

Cakes may be spritzed with brandy or rum and wrapped with cheesecloth, before storing.

Yield: 4, 8 ½ x 4 ½ x 3-inch (21 x 11 x 8 cm) pans

*Deluxe fruit mix consists of candied red and green cherries and pineapple.

DARK FRUITCAKE

Adapted from my mom's recipe, 1972.

1 lb	raisins	454 g
¾ lb	currants	340 g
1 lb	candied cherries, halved	454 g
¾ lb	candied pineapple, chopped	340 g
¼ lb	regular glaze mix or orange and lemon peel	113 g
¼ lb	citron peel	113 g
¼ lb	chopped dates	113 g
½ lb	pecans	227 g
2 cups	unbleached flour	500 mL
1 cup	butter, softened	250 mL
1 cup	granulated sugar	250 mL
5	eggs	5
½ tsp	cloves	2 mL
½ tsp	nutmeg	2 mL
½ tsp	allspice	2 mL
½ tsp	salt	2 mL
1 tsp	cinnamon	5 mL
½ tsp	baking soda	2 mL
Zest	1 lemon	zest
Zest	1 orange	zest
2 Tbsp	lemon juice	30 mL
2 Tbsp	orange juice	30 mL
1 tsp	dried lemon or orange peel	5 mL
½ cup	grape juice	125 mL
¼ cup	blackstrap molasses	60 mL
2 Tbsp	brandy*	30 mL

Preheat oven to 250°F (120°C).

Place first 8 ingredients in large mixing bowl and dredge with 1 cup (250 mL) of the flour. Set aside. Grease 2, 9 x 5 x 3-inch (23 x 13 x 8 cm) loaf pans or line with parchment paper.

In Bosch Universal Kitchen Machine® bowl equipped with cookie paddles, beat butter and sugar. Add remaining ingredients and combine well. Pour floured fruit into mixing bowl and mix well on speed #1. Fill prepared pans ¾ full.

Bake 1 ½–2 hours or until cake tester comes out clean.

Cool on wire rack 20 minutes before removing from pans. Cool completely, wrap and store.

*Exchange 1 tsp orange brandy concentrated extract.

Note: Fruit may be soaked in ¼ cup (60 mL) brandy before mixing with flour.

Yield: 2

FAVOURITE FRUITCAKE

Adapted in 1979, a great way to use mincemeat and candied fruit.

2	eggs	2
1 can	sweetened condensed milk	300 mL
3 cups	mincemeat	750 mL
2 ½ cups	fresh ground whole wheat flour	625 mL
1 tsp	baking soda	5 mL
½ cup	red glazed cherries	125 mL
½ cup	green glazed cherries	125 mL
1 ½ cups	mixed candied fruit	375 mL
1 cup	walnuts, coarsely chopped	250 mL

Preheat oven to 300°F (150°C). Grease large Bundt or tube pan or line 5 medium, 5.75 x 3 x 2-inch (15 x 8 x 5 cm) loaf pans with parchment paper.

In Bosch Universal Kitchen Machine® bowl equipped with cookie paddles, beat eggs, condensed milk and mincemeat.

Add remaining ingredients and mix on speed #1 to combine.

Spread evenly in prepared pans.

Bake in Bundt or tube pan 1 hour and 50 minutes or until cake tester comes out clean.

Bake medium loaves 1 hour and 5 minutes or until cake tester comes out clean.

Cool 10 minutes. Turn out onto wire racks, remove parchment paper and cool thoroughly.

Wrap well in plastic wrap and store in food-safe plastic bags.

Freeze well.

Option: Wrap cooled cakes with a thin layer of marzipan before storing.

If a can has a pull-tab, turn the can over and open the bottom. You will save many spatulas!

MINCEMEAT COFFEE CAKE

Adapted from my friend Gertie's recipe, 1980.

½ cup	butter, softened	125 mL
½ cup	granulated sugar	125 mL
½ cup	brown sugar	125 mL
2	eggs	2
1 ½ cups	mincemeat	375 mL
1 cup	fresh ground whole wheat flour	250 mL
1 cup	unbleached flour	250 mL
2 tsp	baking powder	10 mL
Pinch	salt	pinch
1 tsp	vanilla	5 mL
1 cup	milk	250 mL
¼ tsp	rum extract	1 mL

TOPPING

2 Tbsp	butter, melted	30 mL
2 Tbsp	brown sugar	30 mL
2 tsp	cinnamon	10 mL

Preheat oven to 350°F (180°C).

Cream butter and sugars. Add eggs and mincemeat. Mix well.

Add remaining ingredients and blend to combine.

Pour batter into greased 9 x 9 x 2-inch (23 x 23 x 5 cm) pan.

In small bowl, mix topping ingredients and sprinkle on batter.

Bake 40–50 minutes or until cake tester comes out clean.

Cool on wire rack.

YULE CAKE

My dear friend, Gisele, gave me this recipe in 1986 and we have been enjoying it every year.

¾ cup	unbleached flour	175 mL
½ tsp	baking powder	2 mL
¾ cup	granulated sugar	175 mL
½ tsp	salt	2 mL
3	eggs	3
1 tsp	vanilla	5 mL
1 cup	whole almonds	250 mL
1 cup	whole walnut halves	250 mL
1 cup	whole Brazil nuts	250 mL
8 oz	pitted dates, chopped	250 mL
½ cup	red candied cherries	125 mL
½ cup	green candied cherries	125 mL
½ cup	candied pineapple wedges	125 mL
1 cup	seedless raisins	250 mL

Preheat oven to 300°F (150°C).

In large bowl, sift together dry ingredients over fruit and nuts and toss lightly.

Beat eggs and vanilla in Bosch Universal Kitchen Machine® bowl equipped with cookie paddles and splash ring.

Add remaining ingredients. Cover and pulse momentary switch to combine.

Pour into 4, greased or parchment-lined 5.75 x 3 x 2-inch (15 x 8 x 5 cm) loaf pans.

Bake 1 hour.

Cool in pans 10–20 minutes before removing. Cool completely to store.

Increase baking time to 1 hour and 50 minutes for 2, 8 ½ x 4 ½ x 3-inch (21 x 11 x 8 cm) loaf pans.

Give thanks with a grateful heart.

Yule Cake

GINGERBREAD CAKE

Adapted in 1979.

⅓ cup	granulated sugar	75 mL
1 cup	sifted whole wheat flour*	250 mL
½ cup	barley flour	125 mL
1 ½ tsp	baking powder	7 mL
¾ tsp	baking soda	3 mL
¼ tsp	salt	1 mL
1 ½ tsp	ginger	7 mL
1 ¼ tsp	cinnamon	6 mL
½ tsp	allspice	2 mL
½ cup	buttermilk	125 mL
½ cup	blackstrap molasses	125 mL
¼ cup	butter, softened	60 mL
2	egg whites	2

Preheat oven to 350°F (180°C).

Measure first 9 ingredients into a medium mixing bowl. Stir to blend spices. Add remaining ingredients. Beat until smooth.

Pour into greased 9 x 9-inch (23 x 23 cm) pan.

Bake 25 minutes or until cake tester comes out clean.

Cool on wire rack.

*Sift bran and germ from fresh ground whole wheat flour using a very fine sieve.

CHRISTMAS JEWELS

My dear friend, Gisele, gave me this recipe in 1990. No eggs, sugar or flour required.

6	medium bananas	6
⅔ cup	canola or vegetable oil	150 mL
2 tsp	vanilla	10 mL
¼ tsp	salt	1 mL
3 cups	rolled oats	750 mL
1 cup	oat bran	250 mL
3 cups	mixed fruit, coarsely chopped*	750 mL
1 cup	walnuts or almonds, chopped	250 mL

Preheat oven to 350°F (180°C).

*Chop a mix of dates, apricots, candied cherries and candied fruit.

Mash bananas with oil, vanilla and salt in Bosch Universal Kitchen Machine® bowl equipped with batter whips or cookie paddles. Add remaining ingredients and mix well.

Drop by tablespoonfuls (15 mL) onto greased baking sheets.

Bake 15–20 minutes.

Prep time: less than 5 minutes!

Easy to make. Good fibre and flavour!

CHRISTMAS CAKE COOKIES

Adapted from my friend Catherine's recipe, 1998.

3 cups	dates, chopped	750 mL
2 cups	candied cherries, chopped	500 mL
2 cups	candied pineapple, chopped	500 mL
3 cups	almonds, coarsely chopped	750 mL
3 cups	Brazil nuts, coarsely chopped	750 mL
2 ¼ cups	soft white wheat flour*, divided	560 mL
1 tsp	baking soda	5 mL
1 tsp	salt	5 mL
1 tsp	cinnamon	5 mL
1 cup	butter, softened	250 mL
1 cup	granulated sugar	250 mL
2	eggs	2

Preheat oven to 350°F (180°C).

In a large bowl, mix fruit and nuts in 1 cup (250 mL) of the flour.

In Bosch Universal Kitchen Machine® bowl equipped with cookie paddles, beat butter, sugar and eggs. Add remaining ingredients and mix on speed #1 until combined.

Drop onto greased or parchment-lined baking sheets, about 2 inches (5 cm) apart with 39mm diameter spring-loaded scoop.

Bake 12–14 minutes.

*Soft white wheat flour is whole wheat pastry flour from soft white wheat kernels.

Freeze well.

Yield: 120

A favourite cookie in our home, especially for those who think they don't like fruitcake!

Christmas Cake Cookies, Holiday Fudge and Apricot Balls

Christmas Cake Cookies

GINGERBREAD COOKIES

Adapted in 1980.

½ cup	shortening	125 mL
½ cup	brown sugar	125 mL
1	egg	1
1 cup	blackstrap molasses	250 mL
¼ cup	water	60 mL
3 ¼ cups	unbleached flour	810 mL
¾ tsp	baking soda	3 mL
¼ tsp	cloves	1 mL
½ tsp	cinnamon	2 mL
1 tsp	ginger	5 mL
½ tsp	salt	2 mL

Preheat oven to 350°F (180°C).

Cream shortening and sugar. Beat in eggs, molasses and water.

Add remaining ingredients and mix well. Chill several hours.

Roll on lightly floured surface and cut with cookie cutters. Lift onto baking sheets.

Bake 10–12 minutes.

Decorate as desired.

MINCEMEAT COOKIES

Adapted in 1979 to use the last of the mincemeat.

¼ cup	butter, softened	60 mL
¾ cup	brown sugar	175 mL
2	eggs	2
¾ cup	mincemeat	175 mL
1 ½ cups	fresh whole wheat flour (minus 1 Tbsp)	360 mL
1 ½ tsp	baking soda	7 mL
½ tsp	cinnamon	2 mL
¼ tsp	nutmeg	1 mL
¼ tsp	salt	1 mL
1 ½ cups	semisweet chocolate chips	375 mL
½ cup	walnuts or pecans, chopped	125 mL

Preheat oven to 350°F (180°C).

In Bosch Universal Kitchen Machine® bowl equipped with batter whips or cookie paddles, cream butter and brown sugar.

Add eggs and mincemeat. Mix well.

Add flour, baking soda, cinnamon, nutmeg, salt, chocolate chips and nuts. Pulse momentary switch to combine.

Use 35mm diameter spring-loaded scoop to drop 2 inches (5 cm) apart onto greased or parchment-lined baking sheets.

Bake 8–10 minutes or until golden brown. Cool on wire racks.

Yield: 48

RICE SHORTBREAD COOKIES

Adapted from my mom's recipe, 1972.

2 cups	butter, softened	500 mL
1 ½ cups	confectioner's (icing) sugar	375 mL
1 cup	rice flour	250 mL
3 cups	unbleached flour	750 mL

Preheat oven to 250°F (120°C).

Beat butter and icing sugar very well. Add flours and beat until smooth.

Roll into small balls and place on parchment-lined baking sheets. Press balls gently.

Bake 30 minutes.

Cool on wire racks. Layer between parchment or wax paper to store.

Yield: 90–110

WHIPPED SHORTBREAD COOKIES

Adapted from my mom's recipe, 1972. Melt in your mouth!

1 lb	butter, softened	454 g
1 cup	confectioner's (icing) sugar	250 mL
3 cups	unbleached flour	750 mL
½ cup	cornstarch	125 mL

Preheat oven to 275°F (135°C).

In Bosch Universal Kitchen Machine® bowl equipped with wire whips, beat butter and sugar until light cream colour.

Mix in flour and cornstarch, beating slowly until fluffy.

Use a piping bag or drop by spoonfuls onto baking sheets leaving space between cookies.

Decorate with a piece of candied cherry or small gold or silver ball (dragée) before baking, if desired.

Bake 20 minutes or until golden.

Shortbread cookies are delicious anytime! Why wait for Christmas?

Yule Cake and Rice Shortbread Cookies

CRANBERRY SHORTBREAD COOKIES

Adapted from my mom's shortbread recipe, 1982.

1 ½ cups	unsalted butter, softened	375 mL
3 cups	pastry or fresh ground white wheat flour	750 mL
½ cup	white rice flour	125 mL
¾ cup	granulated sugar	175 mL
Zest	1 orange* (finely grated)	zest
½ cup	dried cranberries, chopped**	125 mL

Preheat oven to 300°F (150°C).

In Bosch Universal Kitchen Machine® bowl equipped with wire whips, pulse butter into pieces.

Add flours, sugar and zest. Pulse momentary switch to evenly distribute ingredients. Add cranberries and pulse to mix.

Gather dough into fist-sized balls and roll each ball into long rolls. Wrap each roll and refrigerate 1 hour.

Remove wrapper, cut into ¼ inch (.64 cm) slices and place on baking sheets.

Bake 15 minutes until pale beige in colour.

*Fresh orange peel may be replaced with 1 teaspoon (5 mL) dried orange peel.

**Chop dried cranberries in food processor or with a sharp knife.

*Dehydrate fresh orange peels. When dry, pulverise in a blender.
Add to breads, baking or cooking recipes, sauces, dips, or as a topping
on icing or salads. Peels add flavour, colour and nutrition!*

SUGAR COOKIES

Adapted from Rena's recipe, 1978. I lived in her home one summer during university and have wonderful memories of the recipes she shared.

1 cup	butter, softened	250 mL
½ cup	granulated sugar	125 mL
1	egg	1
2 tsp	vanilla extract	10 mL
2 ½–3 cups	unbleached flour	625–750 mL
½ tsp	baking powder	2 mL
⅛ tsp	salt	0.5 mL

Preheat oven to 350°F (180°C).

Cream butter and sugar. Beat in egg and vanilla. Add 2 cups (500 mL) flour, baking powder and salt. Cream well. Add remaining flour and beat well.

Wrap and chill dough 1 hour.

Roll ⅛-inch (3 mm) thick on lightly floured surface.

Cut desired shapes and place on baking sheets.

Bake 12–15 minutes.

Cool on wire racks.

Ice and decorate, as desired.

UNBAKED CHOCOLATE DROPS

Adapted from my mom's recipe, 1972.

½ cup	butter	125 mL
2 cups	granulated sugar	500 mL
½ cup	milk	125 mL
6 Tbsp	Dutch cocoa	90 mL
3 cups	quick oats	750 mL
1 cup	long shred coconut	250 mL
½ cup	chopped walnuts	125 mL
Pinch	salt	pinch
1 tsp	vanilla	5 mL

In large saucepan, place butter, sugar and milk. Heat over medium heat stirring often, until boiling. Boil 2 minutes.

Remove pan from heat and add remaining ingredients. Stir well.

Use a spring-loaded scoop to drop onto parchment paper. Cool completely to set.

Cookies may be served or stored when no sticky residue remains on parchment paper.

Store in covered containers between layers of parchment paper.

Yield: 30–36

Quick, easy, and delicious any time of the year!

NANAIMO BARS

Adapted from my sister-in-law Cheryl's recipe, 1980.

BASE

½ cup	butter	125 mL
¼ cup	granulated sugar	60 mL
1	egg	1
5 Tbsp	Dutch cocoa	75 mL
1 tsp	vanilla	5 mL
1 ¾ cups	graham wafer crumbs	425 mL
1 cup	fine coconut, unsweetened	250 mL
½ cup	walnuts, finely chopped	125 mL

Place butter, sugar, egg, cocoa and vanilla in medium stainless or glass bowl. Set bowl over simmering water and stir until butter melts and mixture resembles a thin custard. Remove from heat.

Add wafer crumbs, coconut and walnuts. Blend well.

Pack evenly in greased 9 x 9-inch (23 x 23 cm) pan. Spread filling on base.

FILLING

¼ cup	butter, softened	60 mL
2 Tbsp	vanilla custard powder	30 mL
3 Tbsp	milk	45 mL
2 cups	sifted confectioner's (icing) sugar	500 mL

Cream butter, custard powder and milk.

Beat in icing sugar and spread over base. Set 15 minutes.

ICING

1 Tbsp	butter	15 mL
⅔ cup	chocolate chips	150 mL

Melt chocolate chips and butter. Spread over custard filling.

Set and cut into bars.

Make these bars. Call me! Yum!

LARGE PARTY FUDGE

I created this recipe for a party in 1976.

1 ⅔ cups	evaporated milk	354 mL
4 ½ cups	granulated sugar	1125 mL
1 tsp	salt	5 mL
½ lb	mini-marshmallows	227 g
4 cups	semi-sweet chocolate chips	1000 mL
1 tsp	vanilla	5 mL
1 ½ cups	chopped nuts*	375 mL

Combine milk, sugar and salt in large saucepan over medium heat.

Heat to boiling, cook 5 minutes, stirring constantly. Remove from heat. Add marshmallows and chocolate chips and stir until melted.

Stir in vanilla and nuts.

Spread in parchment-lined 13 x 9 x 2-inch (33 x 23 x 5 cm) pan.

Cool. Lift out of pan to cutting board and cut into squares.

Wrap well to store.

*Exchange chopped cranberries for nuts.

Frozen fudge tastes great!

SWEET AND SAVOURY CANDIED NUTS

Created for a party, 1989.

1 cup	brown sugar	250 mL
1 tsp	salt	5 mL
½ tsp	garlic granules	2 mL
Pinch	cayenne pepper	pinch
1	egg white	1
4 cups	mixed nuts*	1000 mL

Preheat oven to 375°F (190°C).

Mix sugar and spices in small bowl.

In a separate bowl, whisk egg white until frothy. Add nuts and spices. Stir well.

Spread mixture on parchment-lined baking sheet.

Bake 15 minutes until nuts are glazed and sugar is caramelised.

Cool and break into clusters.

*Any combination of pecans, walnuts, raw almonds or hazelnuts.

Prep time: less than 5 minutes!

Yield: 4 cups

A great gift idea!

HOLIDAY FUDGE

Adapted to use candied fruit (I like the cherries), 1989.

1 ½ cups	whipping cream	375 mL
1 cup	light corn syrup	250 mL
¼ cup	butter (no substitute)	60 mL
3 cups	granulated sugar	750 mL
1 cup	red and green candied cherries	250 mL
1 cup	candied pineapple chunks	250 mL
1 tsp	vanilla	5 mL
1 cup	Brazil nuts, chopped	250 mL
1 cup	pecans, chopped	250 mL
1 cup	walnuts, chopped	250 mL

Dipping chocolate (optional)

In large heavy saucepan, combine cream, corn syrup, butter and sugar. Place over medium heat, stirring occasionally until mixture boils.

Use a candy thermometer, cook to soft-ball stage, 234–240°F (112–115°C). Remove from heat and let stand until thermometer reads 200°F (95°C).

Use a mixer to beat fudge until thick and lighter in colour.

Stir vanilla, nuts and fruit into fudge. Mix well.

Spread in parchment-lined 13 x 9 x 2-inch (33 x 23 x 5 cm) pan.

Refrigerate overnight. Lift out of pan and cut into squares.

Wrap well to store.

Option: Exchange candied fruit with dried fruit.

Option: Dip squares in dipping or tempered chocolate and set prior to serving.

Calibrate your candy thermometer at the beginning of each candy-making season.

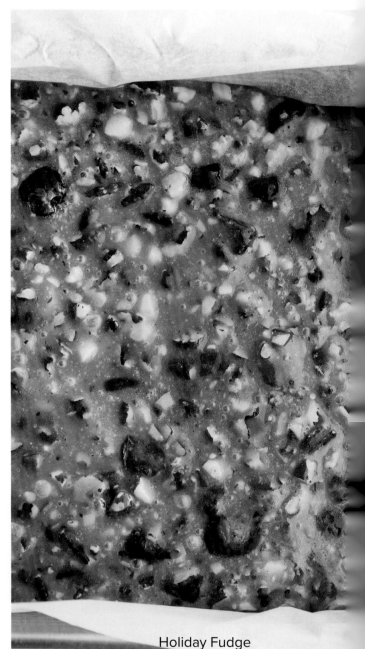

Holiday Fudge

Holiday Fudge

APRICOT BALLS

Adapted in 1986 to add colour and variety to a party platter.

8 oz	dried apricots	227 g
1 cup	flaked coconut, unsweetened	250 mL
¼ cup	sweetened condensed milk	60 mL

Flaked or fine coconut

Chop apricots in a food processor (drop apricots down shoot while blade is turning). Add coconut and continue to process.

Add condensed milk and process to combine.

Shape into small logs or balls. Roll in additional flaked or fine coconut and set on parchment paper until firm.

Store in refrigerator.

Option: Dip *Apricot Balls* in melted dipping or tempered chocolate before rolling in additional coconut.

COCONUT ALMOND BALLS

Adapted to satisfy my sweet tooth, 1986.

7 oz	almond paste or marzipan	200 g
⅓ cup	confectioner's (icing) sugar	75 mL
1 cup	flaked coconut, unsweetened	250 mL
1–2 tsp	water	5–10 mL
7 oz	dipping chocolate	200 g

Line a baking sheet with parchment paper and set aside.

Combine almond paste, sugar and coconut in medium bowl or food processor. Stir in water if mixture appears dry.

Use a spring-loaded scoop to shape balls and place on parchment paper.

Melt chocolate in small bowl over hot water, not boiling, stirring constantly. Or, melt in microwave on 30% power, without a lid, stirring occasionally.

Use a dipping fork to dip balls in melted chocolate.

Return balls to parchment-lined baking sheet and refrigerate until set.

Apricot Balls

CINNAMON SPICED NUTS

Created for gift bags, 1976.

1	egg white	1
1 Tbsp	water	15 mL
1 tsp	salt	5 mL
1 lb	pecans, cashews, walnuts or raw almonds	454 g
⅔ cup	berry (very fine) sugar	150 mL
2 tsp	cinnamon	10 mL
1 tsp	ginger	5 mL
1 tsp	coriander	5 mL

Preheat oven to 275°F (135°C).

Stir sugar and spices in small bowl. Set aside.

In medium-sized bowl, whip all ingredients except nuts. Add nuts and stir well.

Spread on parchment-lined baking sheet.

Bake 50 minutes, stirring twice.

Cool before serving.

Prep time: less than 5 minutes!

SPICED NUTS

Created for gift bags, 1979.

2 cups	pecan halves	500 mL
1 ½ Tbsp	butter, melted	22 mL
1 tsp	salt	5 mL
2 tsp	soy sauce or tamari	10 mL
Dash	Tabasco sauce	dash

Preheat oven to 325°F (160°C).

Mix butter, salt, soy and Tabasco sauce well. Add nuts and stir.

Bake 15–20 minutes, stirring every 5 minutes.

Cool before storing.

Prep time: less than 5 minutes!

Yield: 2 cups (500 mL)

Cinnamon Spiced Nuts

CHRISTMAS FRUIT BREAD

Created in 1986.

4 cups	warm water, 105–115°F (40–45°C)	1000 mL
1–2	eggs	1–2
½ cup	canola or vegetable oil	125 mL
½ cup	granulated sugar	125 mL
1 Tbsp	salt	15 mL
1 ½ cups	regular glaze mix (candied fruit)	375 mL
2 Tbsp	instant yeast	30 mL
10–12 cups	bread or unbleached flour	2500–3000 mL

Pour water, eggs, oil, sugar, salt, glazed fruit and 5 cups (1250 mL) flour into Bosch Universal Kitchen Machine® bowl fitted with dough hook. Position splash ring on bowl and pulse momentary switch to mix gently.

Add ½ cup (125 mL) flour and yeast. Turn to speed #1 and gradually add flour until dough begins to pull away from the side of the bowl. Remove splash ring. Knead 4–5 minutes.

Cover dough and rise 15 minutes. Gently deflate dough with momentary switch. Cover and rise another 15 minutes. Release air from dough and shape on an oiled surface.

Rise until double in volume.

Bake loaves 8 ½ x 4 ½ x 3-inch (21 x 11 x 8 cm) in preheated 350°F (180°C) oven 30 minutes.

Bake braided dough on greased baking sheets in preheated 350°F (180°C) oven 18–20 minutes.

Decorate braided bread with *Icing Sugar Glaze* and glazed red and green cherries.

Transfer to wire rack and cool before storing.

*Exchange melted butter for oil.

Yield: 4 loaves or 3 large braids

OLD-FASHIONED CARROT PUDDING

Adapted from my mom's recipe, 1972.

1 cup	grated raw carrots	250 mL
1 cup	grated raw potatoes	250 mL
1 cup	dry bread crumbs	250 mL
1 cup	raisins, washed	250 mL
1 cup	currants, washed	250 mL
1 cup	brown sugar	250 mL
¾ cup	suet	175 mL
2 Tbsp	sour milk	30 mL
2 tsp	baking soda	10 mL
½ cup	unbleached flour	125 mL
1 tsp	salt	5 mL
1 tsp	cinnamon	5 mL
⅛ tsp	nutmeg	0.5 mL
½ tsp	allspice	2 mL

Stir baking soda into sour milk.

In large bowl, mix all ingredients in the order listed.

Turn mixture into well-greased quart jars or pudding molds, filling half full. Close jars.

Steam (on a trivet) in simmering water 4 hours. Cool and store 3–4 weeks to mellow before serving.

To serve, reheat 30 minutes, on a trivet, in pot of simmering water and ladle *Hard Sauce* over each serving.

HARD SAUCE FOR CARROT PUDDING

2 Tbsp	butter, softened	30 mL
1 cup	confectioner's (icing) sugar	250 mL
2 tsp	vanilla	10 mL
2 Tbsp	brandy, rum or whisky	30 mL
¼ tsp	nutmeg	1 mL
Dash	allspice	dash

Beat butter until creamy. Add sugar and beat well.

Add remaining ingredients and mix.

Spoon sauce over each serving.

TROUBLESHOOTING
(FROM BARB'S EXPERIENCES)

TROUBLESHOOTING –
WHAT HAPPENED TO MY BREAD?

DOUGH DOES NOT RISE BEFORE BAKING

1. Water used for dissolving yeast too cool
2. Dough too stiff
3. Rising area too cool
4. Inactive yeast

BREAD DOES NOT RISE DURING BAKING

1. Forgot yeast
2. Rising area too warm, weakening yeast
3. Dough allowed to rise for too long

CRUST IS TOO THICK

1. Too much flour
2. Insufficient rising
3. Oven temperature too low

BAKED LOAF CRUMBLES EASILY

1. Insufficient kneading
2. Too much flour added
3. Rising area too warm
4. Dough allowed to rise for too long
5. Oven temperature too low
6. Gluten not developed properly

BREAD HAS SOUR TASTE

1. Rising area too warm and dough rose too fast
2. Dough rose for too long before baking

BREAD HAS DARK STREAKS

1. Uneven mixing or kneading
2. Bowl greased too heavily
3. Dough not covered during rising

BREAD HAS HOLES

1. Air not completely pressed from loaves during shaping
2. Overrising before baking
3. Oil and lecithin in the dough – use one or the other.

BREAD DOUGHY ON BOTTOM

1. Bread not removed from pans to cool after baking

BREAD IS WET INSIDE AND COARSE-GRAINED

1. Loaf underbaked
2. Insufficient rising

BREAD IS DRY AND HAS A COARSE GRAIN

1. Too much flour added
2. Dough not kneaded enough
3. Rising period too long
4. Oven temperature too low

TOPS OF BREAD LOAVES CRACK

1. Bread cooled too fast, probably in a draft
2. Dough too stiff
3. Dough not kneaded well

BREAD HAS EXCESSIVE BREAK ON SIDE

1. Oven too hot
2. Insufficient rising
3. Improper shaping

BREAD FALLS IN OVEN

1. Dough was overrisen and got too light

BREAD SMELLS AND TASTES YEASTY

1. Rising time too long
2. Rising area too warm

BREAD DOES NOT BROWN ON SIDES

1. Pans too bright and reflect the heat
2. Poor pan placement or overcrowding in the oven

BREAD IS HEAVY AND COMPACT

1. Too much flour added
2. Dough not allowed to rise enough
3. Whole grain flours may result in heavier (denser) products

BREAD HAS A HOLLOW CAVITY UNDER TOP CRUST

1. Over-risen

BREAD IS TOUGH AND DRY

1. Overbaked
2. Too much flour

TROUBLESHOOTING – WHAT HAPPENED TO MY CAKES?

CAKE RISES AND FALLS IN OVEN

1. Batter overmixed
2. Oven door slammed in the middle of baking

DRY AND CRUMBLY TEXTURE

1. Too much flour
2. Too much gluten in the flour

WET CENTRE

1. Not baked enough
2. Too much liquid
3. Incorrect measurements

DENSE

1. Too much flour
2. Incorrect measurements
3. Ingredients undermixed

DOES NOT RISE

1. Leavening agent not added
2. Inactive (old) leavening

NO FLAVOUR

1. Extracts or flavouring not added
2. Outdated ingredients

RANCID TASTE

1. Outdated ingredients

TOUGH TEXTURE

1. Overmixed

CENTRE NOT BAKED

1. Incorrect oven temperature
2. Oven rack not centred, baking on incorrect level
3. Oven has hot spots
4. Incorrect pan size
5. Incorrect measuring of ingredients
6. Batter not spread evenly
7. Incorrect mixing

EDGES TOO DARK

1. Oven temperature too high
2. Cake overbaked

CAKES CRUMBLES WHEN CUT

1. Using incorrect knife
2. Cake not cooled enough

TROUBLESHOOTING – WHAT HAPPENED TO MY COOKIES?

COOKIES ARE FLAT

1. Overworked dough
2. Incorrect measuring
3. Too much liquid

COOKIES CRUMBLE

1. Too much flour or dry ingredients
2. Not baked enough

DARK EDGES

1. Overbaked
2. Oven too hot
3. Incorrect rack position

TROUBLESHOOTING –
WHAT HAPPENED TO MY MUFFINS?

MUFFINS DON'T RISE

1. Forgot leavening
2. Outdated leavening
3. Over-beaten
4. Not enough batter per muffin cup

DENSE

1. Too much flour
2. Incorrect measurements
3. Undermixed ingredients
4. Over-beaten

CRUMBLE WHEN REMOVED FROM PANS

1. Too much flour
2. Not enough liquid
3. Not baked long enough
4. Removed from pan too quickly

WET CENTRE

1. Too much liquid
2. Not baked long enough

TOUGH

1. Over-beaten

DARK EDGES

1. Overbaked
2. Oven too hot
3. Incorrect rack position

PEAKED SHAPE

1. Overmixed

MUFFINS SPILL OVER PAN

1. Too much leavening
2. Too much batter per muffin cup
3. Overbeaten eggs

RANCID TASTE

1. Outdated ingredients

TROUBLESHOOTING – WHAT HAPPENED TO MY PIE?

PASTRY NOT FLAKY

1. Pastry overworked
2. Not enough fat

TOUGH PASTRY

1. Pastry overworked

PASTRY HAS NO TASTE

1. Forgot salt
2. Old flour

RANCID TASTE

1. Old fat
2. Old flour

DARK EDGES

1. Oven too hot
2. Baked too long

FALL APART WHEN SERVED

1. Cut while hot
2. Improperly prepared pastry

HANDY TOOLS IN BARB'S KITCHEN

Bakeware – personally, I use and recommend professionally trusted USA Pans, made of heavy-gauge aluminized steel, with a fluted surface for even baking. They have a non-stick silicone coating, and are PTFE- and PFOA-free.

Banneton (Brotform) – a proofing (rising) basket which supports dough to maintain shape, preventing sideways spread of moist dough. Dust the basket with flour. The basket yields a better rise and creates a crunchy crust.

Bench Scraper – a rectangular flat piece of stainless steel with a handle along one edge used to separate dough into portions, chop items such as nuts, lift and transfer items, or scrape crumbs from work surfaces. Also called a dough scraper or bench knife. May be plastic.

Brown Sugar Disc – a food safe clay disc used to keep brown sugar soft. Soak in water and place in container of brown sugar. May also be used to rehydrate marshmallows and cookies.

Cake Tester – a long, thin skewer-like stainless steel tool. Insert into the centre of a cake to test if baked. Bake additional time when batter remains on the tester. Clean tester after each use.

Digital Thermometer – a consistent, accurate thermometer used to test liquid and temperature of baked breads, test meats and much more. Not to be used in the oven or microwave.

Docker – a spiky roller with handle, making gentle pricks or holes in pastry or dough, eliminating air pockets as it is rolled across the dough. Usually 3–5 inches wide (7.6–12.7 cm).

Dough Whisk - a long wooden handle with an open spiral for mixing batters, allowing wet and dry ingredients to flow through and not overbeat. Practical for bread dough, including sourdough starters, pizza dough, pancake batter, muffins, soufflés, brownies, granola and so much more. Also called a Danish whisk.

Dry Measure – containers in graduated sizes used to measure dry ingredients. The food can be levelled off with the straight edge of a knife or bench scraper. Also used for measuring thick ingredients such as sour cream or yogurt.

Egg Separator – a tool used to separate the egg yolk and white. The egg yolk remains in the centre cup of the tool and the white slides through slits around the yolk.

Lame – pronounced LAHM, is a razor-sharp blade with a short handle. It is used to score bread dough to control the expansion of the loaf as it rises and bakes, and gives a decorative finish. Also called a baker's blade.

Liquid Measures – containers in graduated sizes used to measure liquid ingredients without spilling.

Oven Liner – a sheet made of non-stick, heat-tolerant food-grade silicone. Collects spills, drips and crumbs.

Oven Thermometer – a thermometer made of stainless steel with a glass lens and markings for Fahrenheit and Celsius. Registers interior oven temperature.

Parchment Paper – a nonstick, cellulose-based composite often used in baking. Grease-, heat- and water-resistant.

Pastry Blender – a stainless steel tool with blades or wires, used to quickly cut shortening, lard or butter into dry ingredients for pastry dough, scones and crumbled toppings.

Rasp – a long, very fine grating tool used to zest citrus fruits, grate fresh nutmeg, garlic, ginger, chocolate or any fine grating. Grates finer than a zester.

Spring-Loaded Scoop – a stainless-steel tool ideal for scooping cookie dough, or use as a meat, fruit and melon baller. Maintains consistent size for even baking and portion control. Available in many sizes.

Zester – a stainless steel tool with sharp etched blades for zesting citrus fruit, grating chocolate, hard cheese, coconut, ginger, nutmeg and other spices. The coloured portion of the peel is called zest, leaving the pale bitter pith.

Baking Log

Date	Page #	Recipe	Comments	Who helped?

When you have completed a recipe, remember and share with a phone shot. Show your friends. Make memories every week!

ACKNOWLEDGEMENTS

Along with my created recipes, some recipes originated from friends and family who I'm thrilled to reference by name and date. Ingredients have been altered and many recipes modified to incorporate fresh ground whole grain flour—always my goal for the health benefits. Thanks for sharing your recipes with me.

A sincere, heartfelt thank-you to friends and family who were willing to taste, offer feedback and ask for second servings. Thank you to my wonderful, loving husband, Tim, for your continued support, encouragement and sense of humour. I love you and I enjoy cooking and baking for you and appreciate your willingness to taste each recipe. Thank you to my friends and family (too many to list) for continually cheering me on, your love, encouragement and input. To all of you, your support has been and always will be invaluable.

To my friends and staff from Barb's (Bosch) Kitchen Centre®, Edmonton (far too many to name), who helped at hundreds of trade shows throughout the years, I appreciate and thank you. Thanks to Geraldine Stefaniuk for over 30 years of assistance prepping the demonstration kitchen for baking and cooking classes at the store. It was always a pleasure to work with you at trade shows and at the store, and travel with you to various speaking engagements. Thanks, Gerry, for all the laughter we shared.

Thank you to those who helped teach cooking classes at Barb's (Bosch) Kitchen Centre® in Edmonton, Alberta, since 1986, and at Red Deer Bosch Kitchen Centre® from 1991–2000, especially my amazing friend, Gisele Bann. I enjoyed teaching with you, and love and appreciate you very much. Thanks for your input while completing this cookbook and for considering this a fun project.

I will be forever grateful for the opportunities through many television invitations, especially to Lorraine Mansbridge, who provided the first invitation. I enjoyed working alongside you very much, value your sincere friendship, love you like a sister, and enjoy sharing life and laughter with you. I am humbled and honoured by your kind words of endorsement and encouragement with this project. Let's bake again soon.

Retail industry does not just happen on its own—there were many company representatives and suppliers who were so important in helping me operate my business successfully. My husband and I developed a close friendship with Bill Marshall, our Zwilling J.A.

Henckels Canada Ltd. representative for over 30 years, and the relationship continues today. Gary Leavitt and the L'CHEF team have been very special to us, personally and professionally, since March 1986. We have a tremendous amount of fun when we are together and we appreciate you very much. Thank you for your consistent support and endorsement.

Thanks to all who have allowed me the privilege to interact with you during classes, provide tips, techniques and instruction, get to know your families, teach your children and grandchildren, and assist you in a positive culinary experience. It was my absolute pleasure to serve, teach and inspire you and your family at Barb's (Bosch) Kitchen Centre® for more than 33 years.

Sincere thank-yous to Jessica Lockert, True Beauty Makeup Artistry, my wonderful daughter-in-law and fantastic makeup artist; amazing photographer and food stylist, Heather Muse; project managers, Anchoby Igot and Rhea Inot; editor, Lara Hyde and the Tellwell team. Working with these wonderful professionals has been a privilege.

From my kitchen to yours, these healthy, tasty and easy recipes are a labour of love, from years of experience, creating and teaching. I'm happy when *you* become comfortable in the kitchen, learn the benefits of healthy homemade food and gain confidence. I encourage you to develop your baking skills, and learn to play in your kitchen, while making priceless memories.

BOSCH™ is a registered trademark of Robert Bosch GmbH, Germany

PRAISE FOR THE BOOK

"Barb's eyes start to dance when she talks of cooking; her joy for food is contagious. That enthusiasm, combined with her knowledge of cooking, made her a delight to welcome on to the set of *ITV's Good, Good Morning*, *Edmonton Live* and *Global Morning News*. I had the absolute pleasure of working with Barb on many TV segments (over three decades!) and was always as thrilled as our viewers were with her cooking and baking ideas and tips. I can't wait to get my hands on a copy of her first cookbook—I know I'll both learn from it and be motivated to try new recipes!"

Lorraine Mansbridge
Host/Producer, *Good, Good Morning with Lorraine Mansbridge*
Anchor/Producer, *Global Morning News*

"Barb has enthusiasm, knowledge and people skills that made her a standout retailer! In the 33 years we did business together, I could always count on her support of the company and products I represented. From cooking classes, knife-sharpening clinics, pie-judging contests and much more, I always had fun and enjoyed calling on her store!"

Bill Marshall
Zwilling J.A. Henckels Canada Ltd. Representative, 1986–2019

"I have known Barb Lockert for more than 30 years, as first a cherished friend and second as a longtime associate in the BOSCH™ mixer business. Barb, along with her husband Tim, began their incredible cooking centre in Edmonton, Alberta, Canada, and steadily improved year after year until it became one of the premier cooking, baking, and teaching centres in all of North America.

Barb's skills at teaching and training are unapparelled. Her love of BOSCH™ and the BOSCH™ mixer set the stage for incredible success as she taught thousands of people from all walks of life to enjoy life and good food. Barb's teaching and training helped better prepare countless families to improve their health and their family enjoyment.

For all of Barb and Tim's success as a BOSCH KITCHEN CENTRE®, it is their humanity and exemplary lives that stand out the most. They have been such great parents, friends, partners, and mentors. They have impacted thousands and thousands of lives for good.

Speaking from a professional view, Barb has been one of the most influential ambassadors for BOSCH™ mixers in the entire world. Because of her teaching and her professional training nearly non-stop for over 30 years, Barb has created a legacy that few have ever, or will ever, achieve.

My sincere congratulations to Barb, to her wonderful husband Tim, and to the creation of this cookbook which will continue to influence many thousands more with her ingenuity and expertise.

I am proud and privileged to call Barb a true friend!"

Gary Leavitt
President, L'CHEF – Exclusive North American
Distributor for BOSCH™ Kitchen Machines

Incredibly yummy recipes in this book include: Unbelievable Whole Wheat Bread (made from freshly ground flour without eggs, sugar, oil or honey), Barb's Carrot Cake, Gerry's Favourite Cookies, Bavarian Apple Torte, Anytime Low-Fat Muffins, Barb's Butter Tarts with a twist, and Christmas Cake Cookies.

INDEX